A STUDY IN THE BOOK OF THE REVELATION

The End time Fulfillment of Bible Prophecy

"And I heard a great voice out of heaven saying, Behold, the tabernacle of God *is* with men, and he will dwell with them, and they shall be his people, and God himself shall be with them, *and be* their God. And God shall wipe away all tears from their eyes; and there shall be no more death, neither sorrow, nor crying, neither shall there be any more pain: for the former things are passed away."

Revelation 21:3-4 (KJV)

M J Tiry

A Study in the Book of the Revelation

The End Time Fulfillment of Bible Prophecy

"And I heard a great voice out of heaven saying, Behold, the tabernacle of God *is* with men, and he will dwell with them, and they shall be his people, and God himself shall be with them, *and be* their God. And God shall wipe away all tears from their eyes; and there shall be no more death, neither sorrow, nor crying, neither shall there be any more pain: for the former things are passed away."

Revelation 21:3-4 (KJV)

ISBN: 979-8-9903305-3-5 Paper Back
ISBN: 979-8-9903305-4-2.Case Bound
ISBN: 979-8-9903305-5-9 ePUB.

Library of Congress Control Number: 2024914940

Print Information Available on the Last Page

ACKNOWLEDGMENTS

If this study in the Revelation is a blessing to the reader, the credit goes to that long line of Bible students whose labor has so benefited me and many others. The studies of men like Clarence Larkin, C. I. Schofield and J Sidlow Baxter who were great students of the Word have been a great help in our understanding of the nature of the present dispensation of grace and the place of Israel in God's plan for the ages. I particularly appreciate the work of the late C. R. Stam of the Berean Bible Society for his studious work in learning and teaching the Word of God. I also have enjoyed and profited from the excellent series of messages by C. Richard Jordan of the Grace School of the Bible on the Book of the Revelation. His insights have helped me much in understanding the structure and layout of this amazing Book of the Revelation. It is my prayer that you the reader will enjoy the study as much as I did in putting it together. I trust that you will also search it out in the Scripture and let the Bible be your final authority.

CONTENTS

Outline of the Revelation

6th Trumpet – 2nd Woe – Four Euphrates angels slay 1/3 of men   9:13-21
    Parenthesis:
    1. The mighty angel came down from heaven   10:1-9
        • Seven thunders uttered their voices (write them not)
        • Stood one foot on land, one on sea (possession of both)
        • Saying there shall be time no more (i.e. times up)
        • When the 7th angel begins to sound, the mystery of God is finished.
    2. The little book 10:8-11
        • John told to eat the book
        • Sweet in mouth but it made the stomach bitter
        • John was to prophecy again before many people, nations, tongues, and kings.
    3. The times of the Gentiles would end in 42 months   11:1-2
    4. The two witnesses   11:3-12
        • They will prophesy 1260 days
        • They are the two olive trees / the two candle sticks
        • Fire from their mouth destroys any who would hurt them
        • They have power:
            o To withhold rain
            o To turn water into blood
            o To smite the earth with plagues
        • When they finish their testimony, the beast that ascends out of the
          bottomless pit will kill them.
        • Their dead bodies lie in the streets of Jerusalem 3 ½ days.
        • After 3 ½ days they are raised by God and stand on their feet. Great fear on
          all who watch.   (vs. 11)
        • They ascend into heaven in a cloud in the sight of their enemies.
    5. There was a great earthquake the same hour they ascended. (vs. 13)
        • 1/10 of the city fell
        • 7,000 men die in the earthquake.
        • The remnant fear and gave glory to the God of heaven.
    The 2nd Woe is past (vs. 14)

7th Trumpet   11:15-19
    In Heaven: Great voices – "the kingdoms of this world are become the kingdoms of
    our Lord, and of is Christ; and he shall reign forever and ever."
        • 24 elders fall on their faces & worship God "We give thee thanks O Lord
          God Almighty, which art, and wast, and art to come: because thou hast taken
          to thee thy great power and hast reigned….the nations were angry and thy
          wrath is come…and the time of the dead that they should be judged… thou
          shouldst reward …the prophets,…the saints …them that fear thy
          name…thou shouldst destroy them that destroy the earth."
        • The temple of God was opened in heaven.   11:19

IV. Seven Personages
    In Heaven
        1. The woman – Israel   12:1&2
            • Cloth with the sun
            • The moon under her feet

- On her head a crown of 12 stars
- Travailed in birth
- Fled to the wilderness to be cared for 1260 days.

2. The Great Red Dragon   12:3&4
- Seven heads and ten horns
- Seven crowns upon his heads
- His tail drew 1/3 of the stars from heaven and cast them to earth
- Stood before the woman which was to be delivered to devour her child as soon as it was born.

3. The man child   12: 5&6
- Was to rule all nations with a rod of iron
- The child caught up unto God and His throne.

4. The archangel   12:7 –
- War in heaven
- Michael and his angels vs. the dragon and his angels
- The dragon defeated (vs. 8)
- The dragon and his angels cast out into the earth (vs. 9)
- The dragon is the devil and the Satan which deceived the whole earth.
- A voice in heaven "Now is come salvation, and strength, and the kingdom of our God, and the power of his Christ: for the accuser of our brethren is cast down, which accused them before our God day and night. And they overcame him by the blood of the Lamb, and by the word of their testimony; and they loved not their lives unto the death…."Therefore, rejoice ye heavens, and ye that dwell in them. Woe to the inhabiters of the earth and of the sea; for the devil is come down unto you, having great wrath because he knoweth that he hath but a little time."   12:10-13

On Earth

5. The Remnant   12:14-17
- The dragon persecuted the woman
- She was nourished for a time and times; and half a time (3.5 years?) in a special place in the wilderness.
- The dragon waged war with the remnant of the woman's seed which keep the commandments of God and love the testimony of Jesus Christ.

6. The Beast out of the Sea   13:1-10
- 7 heads, ten horns, ten crowns, the names of blasphemies
- Like a leopard, feet as of a bear, mouth as a lion,
- The dragon gave him his seat and great authority.
- One head wounded to death but it was healed
- The world wondered and worshipped the dragon
- Given power to continue 42 months

7. The Beast out of the Earth   13:11-18

Parenthesis:

In Heaven
- Vision of the lamb and the 144,000   14:1-5
- Vision of the Angel with the everlasting gospel   14:6-7
- An angel announces the fall of Babylon   14:8

Summary

Things to note from the outline:
- The Book of the Revelation is structured with seven units of seven.
- Each unit of seven (except for the first) starts with action that happens in heaven.
- The action then switches to seven elements of that unit that happens in the earth.
- At irregular intervals in the seven elements of that particular unit, there is a parenthesis which explains
- what just happened in the earth.

PREFACE

One of the campers at Grace Bible Camp one year asked "Who invented the car?" The counselor wisely told him that no one person invented the car – but many people invented the car. It was a step by step process by which the automobile came into existence. One inventor's invention was built on that of inventions by inventors that came before him. The same counselor was also asked "Who started the doctrine of dispensationalism?" Where did this doctrine of "Rightly Dividing the Word of Truth" come from? He again answered wisely saying "It started with the apostle Paul when the Lord Jesus Christ revealed the interruption in Israel's program to start a new dispensation – the dispensation of the grace of God. The sad fact is that the truth of the understanding of the Word of Truth rightly divided was lost to the world at large through the dark ages. The dark ages were dark because the spiritual lights went out for the lack of spiritual understanding. The better question then would have been "When did the recovery of dispensational truth begin?" The answer would be that it started with the protestant reformation. That started a long line of men of God who labored in the Word (the source of all truth) to gain spiritual understanding and knowledge of what God is doing today. Each approached the Bible as absolute truth in which God said what He meant and meant what He said and did so with the conviction that God intended for us to understand it. The result was a long line of genuine Bible students with each recovering more so as to obtain a picture of God's plan for the ages with every increasing clarity while each searched the Word daily whether these things are so. I have great appreciation for these men having enjoyed the blessing of seeing the Word of Truth Rightly Divided.

A word is in order here on how to study the Bible and approach it. Some basic principles are the following:

1. All scripture came from the mouth of God, and it fully equips the man of God to do anything God would have him do. "All scripture is given by inspiration of God, and is profitable for doctrine, for reproof, for correction, for instruction in righteousness: That the man of God may be perfect, throughly furnished unto all good works" (2 Timothy 3:16–17). It can be said that the Holy Spirit never works apart from the Bible and that the Bible never works apart from the Holy Spirit.

2. The term "inspiration of God" in 2Timothy 3:16 means scripture was breath out of God's mouth. It is truly as the Lord tells the devil in Matthew 4:4: "It is written, Man shall not live by bread alone, but by every word that proceedeth out of the mouth of God." And that is the origin of every word of scripture—from the mouth of God.

3. Scripture must be studied in its context to make sense. There are two contexts: the immediate context in which the passage is set and the remote context that looks at the Bible as a whole. Billy Sunday (the great evangelist of the early part of the twentieth century) said, "A text without a context is a pretext." That concept is what Peter was communicating when he said in 2Peter 1:20–21, "Knowing this first, that no prophecy of the scripture is of any private interpretation. For the prophecy came not in old time by the will of man: but holy men of God spake as they were moved by the Holy Ghost." No passage of scripture is intended to stand by itself, but rather each passage actually relates to every other passage of scripture. One of the greatest tools of Bible study is a good cross-reference (e.g., *The Treasury of Scripture Knowledge*). By comparing scripture with scripture, the Bible teaches itself. The Bible itself is its greatest and best teacher.

4. While all scripture is written for our learning, not every passage of scripture is addressed to us. The word of truth then must be "rightly divided." Paul tells us this in 2Timothy 2:15, "Study to shew thyself approved unto God, a workman that needeth not to be ashamed, rightly dividing the word of truth." We direct your attention to Appendix 1.

5. Another key to understanding the Bible is simply to let it mean what it clearly says. It's a major mistake to spiritualize scripture. The Bible is written to be taken literally. There are times when the Bible uses figures of speech (figurative language), but when it does so, it is apparent that such is the

case. Basically, we must remember the adage "If the literal sense makes perfect sense, seek no other sense."

6. God has taken great care to give us His inspired Word and gave it without error. He has also pledged to preserve it so. Psalm 12:6–7 says, "The words of the LORD are pure words: as silver tried in a furnace of earth, purified seven times. Thou shalt keep them, O Lord, thou shalt preserve them from this generation forever." The conviction of this author is that there exists today a preserved text of the inspired and inerrant Word of God. This preserved text is not found in the original manuscripts, since they have been lost through time, but this preservation of scripture exists in the multiplicity of copies. It was God's desire and design that the Bible gets into the hands of the people. If there is a doctrine of preservation, then that preservation is found in the preservation of the scripture in the multiplicity of copies. This author holds the conviction that the preserved text line is the Received Text (Majority Text) of the New Testament and the Masoretic Text of the Hebrew Old Testament. Since there is only one translation in print in English today from these, all scripture quotations in this study are taken from the King James Version of the Bible.

7. There is yet another key to an effective study of the Word of God. That is the heart attitude of the Bereans, described in Acts 17:11. They received the Word with open minds, but they didn't take any man's word for truth or error until they searched it out in the scripture. That approach gave them protection from error, for they made the Word of God their final authority and examined what everyone said based on the Word of truth, the Bible.

8. One final key regarding the Bible having the impact in our lives God intended is to simply believe it. Paul told the Thessalonians that when they received the Word of God, they "received it not as the word of men but as it is in truth the word of God", which "effectually worketh in you that believe." Its not just understanding the Bible that makes it effective, but applying it by faith to one's life makes it effective to give spiritual strength and vitality.   M J Tiry

INTRODUCTION
TO THE BOOK OF THE REVELATION

The Book of the Revelation presents great detail about the period of time in the future that is often called the "Seventieth week of Daniel." It is so called because of an amazing passage in Daniel Chapter 9. In Daniel 9:24 – 27, the angel Gabriel is sent by God to answer Daniel's question regarding what will happen when the seventy years of the captivity of Israel is fulfilled. The seventy years of captivity is foretold in Jeremiah 25:11, "And this whole land shall be a desolation, *and* an astonishment; and these nations shall serve the king of Babylon seventy years."

Daniel had a copy of the Book of Jeremiah and had understanding of the seventy years of captivity from that book (Dan. 9:2). Daniel was praying to the Lord for information as to what will happen now that the seventy years were almost up. Daniel was wondering what will happen when the nation returns to the land. In Daniel Chapter 9, we find Daniel confessing his sins and the sins of the nation. This is exactly what the nation was to do to get out from under the judgment that came upon them because of their disobedience. In Leviticus 26: 14 thru 39 we find five different and successive courses of judgment that would come upon Israel for her sin and rebellion. The first course is in Leviticus 26:14-17. The second is found in verses 18 to 20. The third is in verses 21 and 22 and the fourth is in verses 23 to 26. The fifth course is in verse 27 through 34 and covers the captivity of the nation – which captivity was to last for seventy years. The Book of Daniel documents that captivity. Then in verses 40 on in Leviticus Chapter 26 we find the instructions that the Lord gives to Israel as to how to get out from under the judgment. Note:

> "40 If they shall confess their iniquity, and the iniquity of their fathers, with their trespass which they trespassed against me, and that also they have walked contrary unto me; 41 And *that* I also have walked contrary unto them, and have brought them into the land of their enemies; if then their uncircumcised hearts be humbled, and they then accept of the punishment of their iniquity: 42 Then will I remember my covenant with Jacob, and also my covenant with Isaac, and also my covenant with Abraham will I remember; and I will remember the land. 43 The land also shall be left of them, and shall enjoy her sabbaths, while she lieth desolate without them: and they shall accept of the punishment of their iniquity: because, even because they despised my judgments, and because their soul abhorred my statutes. 44 And yet for all that, when they be in the land of their enemies, I will not cast them away, neither will I abhor them, to destroy them utterly, and to break my covenant with them: for I *am* the LORD their God. 45 But I will for their sakes remember the covenant of their ancestors, whom I brought forth out of the land of Egypt in the sight of the heathen, that I might be their God: I *am* the LORD."
>
> (Lev. 26:40-45)

Israel's History can be traced by following the successive courses of judgment outlined in Leviticus 26. The courses are as follows:
- First course – Consists of the period covered by Judges, Ruth, and 1Samual Chapters 1 through 16.
- The Davidic Kingdom is a bright interlude between the first and the second courses of judgment. As one reads and traces Israel's history through the Old Testament, we see that this period was Israel's golden age as far as her past history is concerned. This Davidic kingdom then became the type of the future kingdom that we see portrayed (prophesied) in the prophets.
- The Second Course consists of the period covered by Elijah's ministry (1Kings 12 to 22).

- The Third Course covered Elisha's ministry (2Kings 1 thru 10:31).
- The Fourth Course covers the events in 2Kings 10:32 to 16:20. This fourth course begins the ministry of the writing prophets. Probably the greatest of the prophets were Elijah and Elisha yet neither of them actually wrote scripture. However, because the coming fifth course will involve God not speaking to Israel, He has the writing prophets write of the glory that is in store for the nation under the reign of the coming Messiah.
- The Fifth Course is presented in 2Kings 17:1 through the end of the Bible (with the exception of the Pauline epistles). This fifth course covers the final segment of the judgment. The Pauline epistles present the body of doctrine called the mystery that was kept secret since the world began but was revealed through Paul. The Pauline epistles do not contain anything on the fulfillment of Old Testament Prophecy but rather presents an interruption of the prophetic program by a secret program that was hid in God from the beginning of the world (Eph. 3:9) but was first revealed to the world through Paul.

  The fifth course is divided into five parts (five sequential steps).

  1. The Assyrian and Babylonian captivities.
  2. The return of a remnant to Jerusalem under the Medes and Persians
  3. The silence of God from Malachi's ministry to John the Baptist
  4. Under Roman rule during the Gospels and Acts

  The Dispensation of Grace is an interruption between the fourth and the fifth parts of the fifth course of judgment.

  5. The Tribulation Period with Israel under the antichrist.

The fifth course finally ends with the return of Jesus Christ to Israel to reign as King of Kings and Lord of Lords. The Book of the Revelation is written to take Israel through the fifth stage of the fifth course. The characteristic of the fifth course is that Israel had lost her sovereignty as a nation and will not get it back until Messiah comes to restore it.

This confessing of his sins and those of his people (See Leviticus 26:40) is what Daniel is doing in Chapter 9 of the book of Daniel. Note Daniel's prayer of confession of the sins of his people Israel:

"5 We have sinned, and have committed iniquity, and have done wickedly, and have rebelled, even by departing from thy precepts and from thy judgments: 6 Neither have we hearkened unto thy servants the prophets, which spake in thy name to our kings, our princes, and our fathers, and to all the people of the land. 7 O Lord, righteousness *belongeth* unto thee, but unto us confusion of faces, as at this day; to the men of Judah, and to the inhabitants of Jerusalem, and unto all Israel, *that are* near, and *that are* far off, through all the countries whither thou hast driven them, because of their trespass that they have trespassed against thee. 8 O Lord, to us *belongeth* confusion of face, to our kings, to our princes, and to our fathers, because we have sinned against thee. 9 To the Lord our God *belong* mercies and forgivenesses, though we have rebelled against him; 10 Neither have we obeyed the voice of the LORD our God, to walk in his laws, which he set before us by his servants the prophets. 11 Yea, all Israel have transgressed thy law, even by departing, that they might not obey thy voice; therefore the curse is poured upon us, and the oath that *is* written in the law of Moses the servant of God, because we have sinned against him. 12 And he hath confirmed his words, which he spake against us, and against our judges that judged us, by bringing upon us a great evil: for under the whole heaven hath not been done as hath been done upon Jerusalem. 13 As *it is* written in the law of Moses, all this evil is come upon us: yet made we not our prayer before the LORD our God, that we might turn from our iniquities, and understand thy truth. 14 Therefore hath the LORD watched upon the evil, and brought it upon us: for the LORD our God *is* righteous in all his works which he doeth: for we obeyed not his voice. 15 And now, O Lord our God, that hast brought thy people forth out of the land of Egypt with a mighty hand, and hast gotten thee renown, as at this day; we have sinned, we have done wickedly. 16 O Lord, according to all thy righteousness, I beseech thee, let thine anger and thy fury be turned away from thy city Jerusalem, thy holy mountain: because for our sins, and for the iniquities of our fathers, Jerusalem and thy people *are become* a reproach to all *that are* about us. [17] Now therefore, O our God, hear the prayer of thy servant, and his supplications, and cause thy face to shine upon thy sanctuary that is desolate, for the Lord's sake. [18] O my God, incline thine ear, and hear; open thine eyes, and behold our desolations, and the city which is called by thy name: for we do not present our supplications before thee for our righteousnesses, but for thy great mercies. [19] O Lord, hear; O Lord, forgive; O Lord, hearken and do; defer not, for thine own sake, O my God: for thy city and thy people are called by thy name."

(Daniel 9: 5-19).

Now let's go to Gabriel's answer to Daniel' prayer.

"[24] Seventy weeks are determined upon thy people and upon thy holy city, to finish the transgression, and to make an end of sins, and to make reconciliation for iniquity, and to bring in everlasting righteousness, and to seal up the vision and prophecy, and to anoint the most Holy. [25] Know therefore and understand, *that* from the going forth of the commandment to restore and to build Jerusalem unto the Messiah the Prince *shall be* seven weeks, and threescore and two weeks: the street shall be built again, and the wall, even in troublous times. [26] And after threescore and two weeks shall Messiah be cut off, but not for himself: and the people of the prince that shall come shall destroy the city and the sanctuary; and the end thereof *shall be* with a flood, and unto the end of the war desolations are determined. [27] And he shall confirm the covenant with many for one week: and in the midst of the week he shall cause the sacrifice and the oblation to cease, and for the overspreading of abominations he shall make *it* desolate, even until the consummation, and that determined shall be poured upon the desolate."

(Daniel 9:24-27)

"Seventy weeks are determined upon thy people." We know from Bible passages such as Genesis 29:27 that a week can be seven years – which is apparently the case here. Gabriel is telling Daniel that though Israel has been in captivity 70 years, that there will be 7 times 70 or 490 years before the kingdom is set up. Now Daniel has a time frame for the setting up of the promised kingdom (i.e. the kingdom of Daniel 2:44).

The bench mark in time is the "going forth of the commandment to restore and rebuild Jerusalem unto Messiah the Prince shall be 69 weeks..." or 483 years. Sir Robert Anderson in his book "The Coming Prince" calculated this and does the mathematics based on the dates of the going forth of that commandment from history. His calculations indicated that the 69 weeks ended on the day that the Lord Jesus Christ rode into Jerusalem on that donkey (John 12:15). Let's consider this amazing prophecy in Daniel. What all will be done at the end of the seventy weeks in Daniel 9:24 include:

1. To finish the transgression…
2. to make an end of sins, (i.e. Israel would stop sinning)
3. and to make reconciliation for iniquity, (God would make reconciliation for the iniquity of Israel's sins. No one then knew how He would do that but it is clearly stated that there would be reconciliation. This we now know referred to the cross.)
4. And to bring in everlasting righteousness, (that is, righteousness conduct will reign on earth when the promised kingdom is established.)
5. and to seal up the vision
6. and prophecy, (The prophetic program will have been fulfilled.)
7. and to anoint the most Holy. (I.e. Israel's Messiah will be reigning on his throne on earth).

Now let's consider that there are several breaks in the 70 weeks. The first break is after the first phase for the rebuilding of the wall. This took seven weeks or 49 years. Then there is a break at the end of the 69th week. After 69 weeks, Messiah is cut off – that is to say that He dies. He dies after the 69th week but they do not have enough information to figure that out yet at the time that it was written. Even His apostles could not figure that out as is evident from passages such as Luke 18:34 and in Matthew 16: 22 where we find Peter rebuking the Lord for saying that He would be killed and be raised again the third day. It is apparent for us looking back at it that there is an interruption between the end of the 69th week and the beginning of the seventieth (see verse 26 in the Daniel 9 passage) However, the duration of the interruption is not specified in Daniel Chapter 9. The duration of that interruption is stated by the Lord in Luke 13:8 (the parable of the Fig Tree and the three years of the Lord's ministry to Israel) where He defines the break between the end of the 69th week and the beginning of the 70th as being another year. We note that the vine dresser in the parable in Luke 13 is the Holy Spirit. THe words "Lord, let it alone this year also…" defines for us the time between the ascension of the Lord to Heaven and the stoning of Stephan. This interruption is for the purpose of God making the official offer of the Kingdom to Israel which happened in the first seven chapters of the Book of Acts. This year is a part of what Isaiah called "the acceptable year of the Lord" (Isa. 61:2) when Israel was being called to the Kingdom by the witness of the Holy Ghost at Pentecost. Israel, through her leaders, had rejected the appeal of God the Father that He made through John the Baptist (Matt. 21:25). They did the same with Christ during His earthly ministry to the nation (John19:15). Now, in the first chapters of the Book of Acts, those same leaders will have another opportunity to receive that Kingdom by repenting of their deed of crucifying their Messiah.

After His death, burial and resurrection and ascension back to heaven, the Lord would sit at the Father's right hand until the Father makes His enemies His footstool (Psa. 110:1; Matt. 22:44; and Heb. 1:13). One year later (one year after His ascension back to heaven), we come to the stoning of Stephen. Stephen is found prophetically in the parable in Luke 19:14. Stephen is the messenger in that parable that the nation sends to tell the Lord that they will not have Christ to reign over them. The sentiments of the hard hearted nation are expressed in the words of Luke 19:14 " But his citizens hated him, and sent a message after him, saying, We will not have this *man* to reign over us."

An understanding of the two parables (in Luke Chapters 13 and 19) cited above are important in gaining a discernment of what is happening in the Book of Acts and to see the crisis point that Israel is at in her national history. To put them in perspective though, we go to Acts Chapter 7 and Stephen's address to the nation.

In Acts 7: 41-47, he calls them to remember that the nation had gone so far into idolatry that God had to give them up and take them into captivity in Babylon. He further points to the fact that God drove out the Gentile nations who possessed the land before them that it might be their land. He calls them to remember the victories of the nation under David and the glory of Solomon's reign.

Acts 7:48-53

"[48] Howbeit the most High dwelleth[h] not in temples made with hands; as saith the prophet, [49] Heaven *is* my throne, and earth *is* my footstool: what house will ye build me? saith the Lord: or what *is* the place of my rest? [50] Hath not my hand made all these things? [51] Ye stiffnecked and uncircumcised[i] in heart and ears, ye do always resist the Holy Ghost: as your fathers *did*, so *do* ye. [52] Which of the prophets have not your fathers persecuted? and they have slain them which shewed before of the coming of the Just One; of whom ye have been now the betrayers and murderers: [53] Who have received the law by the disposition of angels, and have not kept *it*."

He calls them here to think on the temple and to point out that they make much of the temple (which he was accused of blaspheming) but they do not truly worship the God of the temple. They were circumcised outwardly but uncircumcised in heart and ears. He points out that they (or their predecessors) had persecuted the prophets who spoke of the coming of Christ and now have actually been the murderers and betrayers of their Messiah. What an indictment! He goes further to point out their hypocrisy of having received the Law (which he is also accused of them as blaspheming) and had not kept it. The point that he is making is that the nation had a long history of disobedience to God and that they as the leaders of the nation were continuing in the footsteps of their predecessors

Stephen refers to them as "Uncircumcised in heart and ears…" Paul the apostle talks about such Jews in Romans 2:29 saying "For he is not a Jew, which is one outwardly; neither *is that* circumcision, which is outward in the flesh: But he *is* a Jew, which is one inwardly; and circumcision *is that* of the heart, in the spirit, *and* not in the letter; whose praise *is* not of men, but of God." The Jew who is circumcised in heart is one who listens to what God had to say and then follows it by faith that is put into action (James 2:22).

Acts 7:54-60

"54 When they heard these things, they were cut to the heart[j], and they gnashed on him with *their* teeth. 55 But he, being full of the Holy Ghost, looked up stedfastly into heaven, and saw the glory of God, and Jesus standing[k] on the right hand of God, 56 And said, Behold, I see the heavens opened, and the Son of man standing on the right hand of God. 57 Then they cried out with a loud voice, and stopped their ears, and ran upon him with one accord, 58 And cast *him* out of the city, and stoned *him*: and the witnesses laid down their clothes at a young man's feet, whose name was Saul[l]. 59 And they stoned Stephen, calling upon *God*, and saying, Lord Jesus, receive my spirit. 60 And he kneeled down, and cried with a loud voice, Lord, lay not this sin to their charge. And when he had said this, he fell asleep."

He finally manages to bring the leaders of Israel to the point of conviction. Unfortunately, their conviction did not lead to repentance but rather it led them to such an angry rage that they stopped their ears so that can not hear any more and then proceeded to kill him.

In verse 55 Stephen sees the Lord standing at the right hand of God. This is a most significant posture for the Lord to take at this time. Remember that in Acts 2:34 Peter quotes the 110th Psalm about the Lord sitting at the right hand of God until it is time to make His enemies His footstool. The fact that the Lord is seen by Stephan as standing is an indication that the time had come for Him to do just that – to make His enemies His foot stool. The seventy weeks of Daniel Chapter Nine comes into memory here. We understand and can see from the narrative in Daniel 9 that there was a break in the prophetic action between the end of the 69th week and the beginning of the seventieth. In Luke 13:8 we see what the duration of the break actually was – "Let it alone this year also." That year is now up (at this point in the Book of Acts) with the stoning of Stephen. It is time for the Lord to now return and bring the seventieth week – the tribulation period (Psalm 7:6; 9:19 & 20). Christ indeed does return. However, He does not return to bring the tribulation (the time of His wrath) but to save the leader of Israel's rejection of Him – Saul of Tarsus. What a testimony of the love, the grace, mercy and peace of God.

Let's consider the passage in Luke 13 in some detail as it bears on this event (the stoning of Stephen) heavily:

Luke 13:1-9 (KJV)

1 There were present at that season some that told him of the Galilaeans, whose blood Pilate had mingled with their sacrifices. 2 And Jesus answering said unto them, Suppose ye that these Galilaeans were sinners above all the Galilaeans, because they suffered such things? 3 I tell you, Nay: but, except ye repent, ye shall all likewise perish. 4 Or those eighteen, upon whom the tower in Siloam fell, and slew them, think ye that they were sinners above all men that dwelt in Jerusalem? 5 I tell you, Nay: but, except ye repent, ye shall all likewise perish. 6 He spake also this parable; A certain *man* had a fig tree planted in his vineyard; and he came and sought fruit thereon, and found none. 7 Then said he unto the dresser of his vineyard, Behold, these three years I come seeking fruit on this fig tree, and find none: cut it down; why cumbereth it the ground? 8 And he answering said unto him, Lord, let it alone this year also, till I shall dig about it, and dung *it*: 9 And if it bear fruit, *well*: and if not, *then* after that thou shalt cut it down.

The fig tree when used figuratively in scripture represents religious activity. Remember that it was fig leaves that Adam and Eve used to cover their nakedness when they knew they were naked. The vineyard represents Israel as a nation in scripture (Isa. 5:4 & 5; Mat. 21:40; etc.).The three years spent seeking fruit was the three years of the Lord's public ministry to Israel. The religious system of Israel (represented figuratively by the fig tree) did not produce fruit – that fruit being their trust in Christ as Messiah. The Lord then would have cut it down but the vine dresser (that being the Holy Spirit) says he will dung it and hoe about it and give it another year. That one year turns out to be the time interval between the crucifixion and the stoning of Stephen. With the stoning of Stephen, Israel as a nation is committing the unpardonable sin of blaspheming the Holy Spirit (Mat. 12:31).

There is another parable that the Lord spoke to Israel that comes into play here. That is in Luke 19:12.

> **Luke 19:11-27 (KJV)** [11] And as they heard these things, he added and spake a parable, because he was nigh to Jerusalem, and because they thought that the kingdom of God should immediately appear. [12] He said therefore, A certain nobleman went into a far country to receive for himself a kingdom, and to return. [13] And he called his ten servants, and delivered them ten pounds, and said unto them, Occupy till I come. [14] But his citizens hated him, and sent a message after him, saying, We will not have this *man* to reign over us. [15] And it came to pass, that when he was returned, having received the kingdom, then he commanded these servants to be called unto him, to whom he had given the money, that he might know how much every man had gained by trading. [16] Then came the first, saying, Lord, thy pound hath gained ten pounds. [17] And he said unto him, Well, thou good servant: because thou hast been faithful in a very little, have thou authority over ten cities. [18] And the second came, saying, Lord, thy pound hath gained five pounds. [19] And he said likewise to him, Be thou also over five cities. [20] And another came, saying, Lord, behold, *here is* thy pound, which I have kept laid up in a napkin: [21] For I feared thee, because thou art an austere man: thou takest up that thou layedst not down, and reapest that thou didst not sow. [22] And he saith unto him, Out of thine own mouth will I judge thee, *thou* wicked servant. Thou knewest that I was an austere man, taking up that I laid not down, and reaping that I did not sow: [23] Wherefore then gavest not thou my money into the bank, that at my coming I might have required mine own with usury? [24] And he said unto them that stood by, Take from him the pound, and give *it* to him that hath ten pounds. [25] (And they said unto him, Lord, he hath ten pounds.) [26] For I say unto you, That unto every one which hath shall be given; and from him that hath not, even that he hath shall be taken away from him. [27] But those mine enemies, which would not that I should reign over them, bring hither, and slay *them* before me.

The nobleman in this parable in Luke 19 is the Lord Jesus Christ. He goes to a far country (i.e. he returns to heaven) to receive the kingdom. His citizens (the leaders of Israel who represent the nation at large) hated Him and sent a messenger after Him saying "we will not have this man to reign over us." Christ's citizens were the citizens of Israel. The messenger that they sent was Stephen. The servants were the believing remnant of Israel. The number ten is significant in that it represents the Gentiles. Each servant was given a pound. Between the time that the Lord leaves to receive the kingdom (i.e. to return to heaven and then return to earth with the kingdom) the servants will be ministering the gospel of the kingdom to the Gentiles. This will be the activity of the believing remnant of Israel in the coming Tribulation period. There is an obvious purpose for this parable – that being to give Israel hope and understanding when the kingdom did not immediately appear.

So now with the stoning of Stephen we would expect the 70th week to come in by which the Lord would make His enemies His footstool. Instead though, something wonderful and totally un-prophesied happened. It was something that God that God had in mind from before the foundation of the world but which He had hid in Himself (Eph. 3:3-6). He revealed the mystery program in which He calls out from among the Gentiles (which now includes Israel as being just another nation among the nations) a body of believers that He would save by grace through faith apart from the Law, apart from human merit, and apart from Israel. God changed the elect agency that He is using in the salvation of souls. Now during the dispensation of grace, the elect agency will be the church which is Christ's body. It is a Gentile church though Israelites can become members of it. The nation of Israel is no longer (as long as the dispensation of grace continues) the agency for saving souls.

God stopped the prophetic clock and interrupted the prophetic program again in the saving of Saul of Tarsus. This is the second interruption in the seventy weeks -- the gap between the 69th week and the 70th week with the year of Luke 13:8 being the first. The seventieth week is now postponed until a time in the future after the mystery program will have run its course (2Thess. 2:5-8). This will happen when the event that we call the rapture closes the mystery program (the dispensation of the grace of God) and takes the church the body of Christ to its eternal home in heaven (2Cor. 5:1).

Through the saving of Saul of Tarsus and the revelation of the mystery concerning the Gentile program called in scripture "the dispensation of the grace of God," God revealed the fact that He has a twofold purpose that he is working out in time. It is actually a reconciling ministry whereby He will reconcile every thing in heaven and in earth back to Himself. He will reconcile the heavens to Himself through "the church which is Christ's Body" (Eph. 5:23; Col. 1:18; 1:24-26) by means of a program of salvation called "the preaching of Jesus Christ according to the revelation of the mystery." (Rom. 16:25; 1Tim. 3:16) He interrupted the prophetic program to introduce, execute, and consummate the mystery program.

I offer the following passage from Colossians for the reader's consideration here. It is profound in its scope regarding the eternal purpose for man in God's plan for the ages and it ties the two programs (the prophetic program concerning Israel and the mystery program concerning the Gentiles regarding the Body of Christ) into one overall program hereby every thing in heaven that is created by Christ and for Christ and every thing in earth are reconciled to God by His redeeming work of Calvary.

> **Colossians 1:12-29 (KJV)** [12] Giving thanks unto the Father, which hath made us meet to be partakers of the inheritance of the saints in light: [13] Who hath delivered us from the power of darkness, and hath translated *us* into the kingdom of his dear Son: [14] In whom we have redemption through his blood, *even* the forgiveness of sins: [15] Who is the image of the invisible God, the firstborn of every creature: [16] For by him were all things created, that are in heaven, and that are in earth, visible and invisible, whether *they be* thrones, or dominions, or principalities, or powers: all things were created by him, and for him: [17] And he is before all things, and by him all things consist. [18] And he is the head of the body, the church: who is the beginning, the firstborn from the dead; that in all *things* he might have the preeminence. [19] For it pleased *the Father* that in him should all fulness dwell; [20] And, having made peace through the blood of his cross, by him to reconcile all things unto himself; by him, *I say*, whether *they be* things in earth, or things in heaven. [21] And you, that were sometime alienated and enemies in *your* mind by wicked works, yet now hath he reconciled [22] In the body of his flesh through death, to present you holy and unblameable and unreproveable in his sight: [23] If ye continue in the faith grounded and settled, and *be* not moved away from the hope of the gospel, which ye have heard, *and* which was preached to every creature which is under heaven; whereof I Paul am made a minister; [24] Who now rejoice in my sufferings for you, and fill up that which is behind of the afflictions of Christ in my flesh for his body's sake, which is the church: [25] Whereof I am made a minister, according to the dispensation of God which is given to me for you, to fulfil the word of God; [26] *Even* the mystery which hath been hid from ages and from generations, but now is made manifest to his saints: [27] To whom God would make known what *is* the riches of the glory of this mystery among the Gentiles; which is Christ in you, the hope of glory: [28] Whom we preach, warning every man, and teaching every man in all wisdom; that we may present every man perfect in Christ Jesus: [29] Whereunto I also labour, striving according to his working, which worketh in me mightily.

Every word in every verse in this passage is significant in the reconciling ministry of Christ in His creation:
- Verse 12 -- The Father made every believer fit to be a part of the inheritance that is Christ's.

- Verse 13 -- Every believer was translated from the power of darkness into the kingdom of His Son.
- Verse 14 -- Every believer is redeemed by His blood.
- Verse 15 – Jesus Christ is the visible manifestation of the God that otherwise could not be seen.
- Verse 16 – He (Jesus) is the creator of all things and the ruling authority of it in heaven and in earth.
- Verse 17 – He was there before there was anything (John 1:1-4), and He holds all things together by the power of His will.
- Verse 18 – He is the head of the church the Body of Christ and is the first to rise in resurrection life that He might be preeminent in all things that are created by Him and for Him.
- Verse 19 -- It pleased the father that all fullness dwell in Him.
- Verse 20 – He made peace through the blood of His cross to reconcile everything in heaven and earth to Himself.
- Verses 21 -- He personally reconciled every believer so that each might be holy, unblamable, and unreprovable in His sight.
- Verse 22 – He did that in the body of His flesh through death.
- Verse 23 – He did that by the hope of the gospel of which Paul was made a minister.
- Verses 24 – Paul rejoiced in what sufferings he endured so the Body of Christ could have the message of grace.
- Verse 25 – The gospel which Christ gave to Paul completed the word of God. Adding the mystery to the Bible completed the cannon of scripture. The cannon of scripture is now closed.
- Verse 26 – The message that was once hid from all in now revealed to all.
- Verse 27 -- God desires that the riches of the glory of this mystery be known by all.
- Verse 28 – Paul labored to bring all men to maturity in Christ through that message.

It is significant that Saul of Tarsus comes on the scene at the stoning of Stephan (Acts 7:58). Saul was leading Israel's rejection of Christ (Acts 8:3). But Jesus Christ saves Saul on the road to Damascus (Acts 9:4-15) and makes him the pattern "...for them which should hereafter believe on him to life everlasting." (1Tim. 1:16)

There is yet one more consideration of what happened with the saving a Saul of Tarsus that adds depth to the riches of the grace that underpins the dispensation of grace. That is the fact that Saul committed the unpardonable sin along with the rest of the leaders of Israel. Yet he became a saved man. We noted above how it was the outreach of the Holy Spirit of God through Peter and the twelve apostles at Pentecost in Acts Chapter 2 that Saul rejected. To understand how it is that Israel was at her crisis point in the first chapters of Acts, we go to the Lord's word to Israel in Matthew 12:31-32 "Wherefore I say unto you, All manner of sin and blasphemy shall be forgiven unto men: but the blasphemy *against* the *Holy* Ghost shall not be forgiven unto men. And whosoever speaketh a word against the Son of man, it shall be forgiven him: but whosoever speaketh against the Holy Ghost, it shall not be forgiven him, neither in this world, neither in the *world* to come."

Saul of Tarsus became a saved man the only way someone who committed the unpardonable sin could get saved – that was for God to start a new dispensation in which there is no unpardonable sin. Saul of Tarsus became the first member of the Body of Christ and the first person to be saved by grace in the dispensation of grace. In fact we now can understand that the dispensation of grace started with the saving of Saul. He therefore could write to Timothy: "This *is* a faithful saying, and worthy of all acceptation, that Christ Jesus came into the world to save sinners; of whom I am chief. Howbeit for this cause I obtained mercy, that in me first Jesus Christ might shew forth all longsuffering, for a pattern to them which should hereafter believe on him to life everlasting." (1Timothy 1:15-16) He is the pattern of how people are saved today in the dispensation of grace because it started with his salvation. Everyone saved since then has been saved on the same basis as he was – by grace through faith apart from works and apart from Israel's program of prophecy. That will be the pattern until the Lord closes the dispensation of grace.

One day the temporary interruption between the 69th and the 70th weeks will be over. When that time comes, the prophetic program will pick up where God left off with it. When that happens, the portion of Scripture that we know as Hebrews though Revelation will give Israel the information that she needs to go through the last days – the seventieth week of Daniel Chapter 9. This Book of the Revelation outlines the events of the seventieth week.

Study Guide Questions on the Introduction

1. What did Daniel (Dan. 9:2) learn from Jeremiah the prophet (Jer. 25:11) about the captivity of Israel?

2. Leviticus 26:14-39 lays out five courses of judgment that would come on Israel if they failed to keep the law. List those courses and the Old Testament scripture to document them.

3. Leviticus 26: 40 – 45 lists what Israel would have to do to get out from under that fifth course -- the captivity. What do we find Daniel doing relative to that in Daniel 9:5-19?

4. What was Daniel hoping to see happen once the 70 year captivity ends? What did Gabriel tell Daniel would happen? (Dan 9: 24-27)?

CHAPTER 1

The Book of the Revelation basically covers the seventieth week of Daniel Chapter 9. It does however; extend out through the millennial reign of our Lord Jesus Christ and into His eternal Kingdom. It concludes with the new heaven, the new earth and the New Jerusalem. It therefore encompasses the communication of God's plan to reconcile all things in heaven and in earth back to Himself (Col. 1:16).

"The Revelation of St. John the Divine" - This is the tile of the book. "The divine" = the discerner, the one who received the revelation (see Genesis 44:15 and Acts 16:16 on the meaning of the term "divine")

The Revelations of Jesus Christ

Revelation 1:1&2

"¹The Revelation of Jesus Christ which God gave unto him, to shew unto his servants things which must shortly come to pass; and he sent and signified *it* by his angel unto his servant John: ² Who bare record of the word of God, and of the testimony of Jesus Christ, and of all things that he saw." (Rev 1:1&2)

Note in verse 2 "…of all things that he saw." When John wrote the book, he had already seen in visions everything that he wrote in the book. In verse 10 he tells us where he got the information. God gave it, Jesus Christ sent it, the angel signified it (i.e. revealed it in signs), John wrote it, and the servants (the remnant of Israel) received it (or were to receive it). It reveals the glory of Christ. These things must shortly (quickly) come to pass. (Rev. 22:10, 12, 20)

- The Subject of the Book is "The Revelation of Jesus Christ." The Book of the Revelation is the revelation of Jesus Christ to John. This is the revelation of Jesus Christ in Glory. When He came the first time, He came to earth to go to the cross to accomplish redemption for us. He received what was due to us – He endured God's wrath against sin. When He comes the second time, He will get what is rightfully due Him as the creator of all things (Heb. 1:2; 12:2; Col. 1:16-20) and the redeemer of man.
- Philippians Chapter 2 tells of His mindset in enduring the cross: "⁵Let this mind be in you, which was also in Christ Jesus: ⁶ Who, being in the form of God, thought it not robbery to be equal with God: ⁷ But made himself of no reputation, and took upon him the form of a servant, and was made in the likeness of men: ⁸ And being found in fashion as a man, he humbled himself, and became obedient unto death, even the death of the cross. ⁹ Wherefore God also hath highly exalted him, and given him a name which is above every name: ¹⁰ That at the name of Jesus every knee should bow, of *things* in heaven, and *things* in earth,
- and *things* under the earth; ¹¹ And *that* every tongue should confess that Jesus Christ *is* Lord, to the glory of God the Father." (Phil. 2:5-11)
- The servants in verse 1 are Israelites (Isa. 43:10; 46:13 cf 48:11; 65:8&9, 13-15; Rev. 2:20;19:2; 22:6; 7:1; Lev. 25:55; Isa. 49:3; Rev. 1:6). God shall call His servants by another name – they will be called "Kings and priests" (Rev. 1:6; 5:10; Exod. 19:5&6; Isa. 61:6).
- God's servant (the remnant) is the reason why the nation was not destroyed (Isa. 65:8-15 & 65:15)

Blessed is he that reads and keeps

Revelation 1:3

"Blessed *is* he that readeth, and they that hear the words of this prophecy, and keep those things which are written therein: for the time *is* at hand." (Rev 1:3)

Observe:

- The Book is a book of prophecy – it is future. Prophecy is not being fulfilled today during the dispensation of grace. We today live under the preaching of Jesus Christ according to the revelation of the mystery (Rom. 16:25).
- "The time is at hand …"– 1Peter 4:7 cf 2Peter 3:15-16. Note that Peter, James and John learned about the interruption in the prophetic program through Paul (Gal. 2:7-10). It is clear from information contained in the Book of the Revelation that John did not know of the revelation of the mystery yet at the time that he wrote the Revelation. Therefore, the book of the Revelation would have had to have been written before Acts 15. We would therefore place this writing of the Revelation around AD 47.
- Note in verse 2 that John wrote of all things that he saw. John had already seen everything that is written in this book. This introduction was written after the book itself was written.
- Four ways that people see and/or study the Book of the Revelation:
  1. Prederist View –This view holds that it is all history by 350 AD
  2. Historical View – It is a picture of the history of the church which is Christ's Body.
  3. Semi futurist view – Some of it is history and some prophecy (Schofield's view)
  4. All of the events described in the Revelation are future from the present dispensation of grace – This is the view presented in this study.

The Seven Churches in Asia

Revelation 1:4a

"John to the seven churches which are in Asia:" (Rev 1:4)

The seven churches in Asia have some significance in the ministry to the circumcision:

- In Galatians 2:9 the twelve were going to limit their ministry to the circumcision. Therefore, the seven churches are part of the circumcision. These churches are not a part of the church which is Christ's Body. There are three different churches mentioned in the New Testament Scriptures (Eph. 1:22, Acts 7:38, Matt. 16:18). A church is a called out assembly of believers – called out of a larger group for a specific purpose or a destiny. When we see the word "church" we need to ask ourselves four questions:
  1. What is the larger group from which it is called out?
  2. What is the identity of the smaller, called out group?
  3. What is the basis on which the group is called out?
  4. What is the called out group called to?

- Let's apply those questions to these three different churches referred to in the New Testament Scriptures:
  1. The church in the wilderness (Act 7:38) consists of the nation of Israel which was called out of Egypt to go into the Promised Land. It was called out on the basis of the Abrahamic Covenant by which God would give the land of Palestine to Israel – Abraham's seed.
  2. The church in Matthew 16:18 is the believing remnant of Israel called out of the unbelieving nation of Israel to go into the Promised Kingdom. This is the Little Flock of Luke 12:32. That church will be called out based on the confession that Jesus is the Christ, the Son of the living God.
  3. The church in Ephesians 1:22 is the church which is Christ's body – a body of believers called out of the lost masses of humanity today in the dispensation of grace to be the means whereby it becomes the elect agency by which God reconciles the things in the heavenly places to Himself. There are local churches of both the Body of Christ and the Messianic church (Heb. 10:24). These churches in Asia are circumcision churches and are a part of the Messianic church that the Lord referred to in Matthew 16: 18.

- Why seven? Seven is the number of perfection or completion. These seven letters give to Israel the totality of the instructions that the nation will need to get through the tribulation period and into the kingdom.

- Why Asia?
    1. The church at Jerusalem was scattered (Acts 8:1).
    2. Note that James writes to the twelve tribes scattered (James 1:1).
    3. Note also that Peter writes to the strangers scattered throughout Asia (1Peter 1:1) - the location of the seven churches of Revelation Chapters 2 and 3.
    4. Paul (the apostles of the Gentiles) was forbidden (temporarily) to go to Asia where these circumcision churches existed (Acts 16:6). Later however, Paul carried on a ministry there. John (the apostle) was ministering to these seven circumcision churches at that time in which Paul was forbidden to minister there. Likely the Book of the Revelation was being written during that time. This would be about 47 AD.
    5. Revelation 2:9 "those that say they are Jews and are not..." indicates that these are Jewish churches.
    6. Satan's seat is there in Asia according to Revelation 2:13.

Revelation 1:4b

"Grace *be* unto you, and peace, from him which is, and which was, and which is to come; and from the seven Spirits which are before his throne;" (Rev 1:4)

These greetings are from:
- Him which is, and which was and which is to come – that is in reference to Christ.
- The Seven Spirits of God are seen in Isaiah 11:1 & 2 as seven spirits that rest upon Christ as the stem of Jesse. These seven spirits are characteristics of Christ. They are: 1. The Spirit of the Lord, 2. the spirit of wisdom, 3. the spirit of understanding, 4. the spirit of counsel, 5. the spirit of might, 6. the spirit of knowledge, and 7. the fear of the Lord.
- These seven Spirits belong to Christ (Rev 3:1)
- These are further represented by the seven lamps before God's throne (Rev. 4:5)
- In Revelation 5:6 the lamb has seven horns and seven eyes which are these seven Spirits that characterize Christ.

Jesus the Prophet, Priest and King

Revelation 1:5

"And from Jesus Christ, *who is* the faithful witness, *and* the first begotten of the dead, and the prince of the kings of the earth. Unto him that loved us, and washed us from our sins in his own blood,"

And from Jesus, who is:
- o The faithful witness – He is a Prophet
- o The first begotten from the dead (Acts 13:33; Heb 1:5) – He is a Priest
- o Prince of the kings of the earth – He is the rightful King of planet earth.

Israelites made to be Prophets, Priests, and Kings

Revelation 1:6-9

"[6]And hath made us kings and priests unto God and his Father; to him *be* glory and dominion for ever and ever. Amen. [7] Behold, he cometh with clouds; and every eye shall see him, and they *also* which pierced him: and all kindreds of the earth shall wail because of him.

Even so, Amen. [8] I am Alpha and Omega, the beginning and the ending, saith the Lord, which is, and which was, and which is to come, the Almighty. [9]I John, who also am your brother, and companion in tribulation and in the kingdom and patience of Jesus Christ, was in the isle that is called Patmos, for the word of God, and for the testimony of Jesus Christ." (Rev 1:6-9)

In the Gospel of John 21:21- 23 we see an interesting statement that is meaningful when we read the Book of the Revelation. The Lord tells Peter with reference to John "If I will that he tarry till I come, what is that to thee?..." Verse 23 clarifies this saying that this did not mean that he would not die but that he will tarry until Christ comes. The Lord had in view here the fact that John would see the Lord's return in spirit so that he could write the account of it in the Book of the Revelation. John was their companion in tribulation (verse 9) because he went through it with them in the spirit. John was sent by Christ to the isle of Patmos to receive the Revelation. James and John were surnamed the sons of thunder. Thunder is associated with the voice of God. There is a reason why James was targeted in Acts 12:1&2. Moses completed the Law, John completed prophecy, and Paul completed the Word of God with the mystery (Col. 1:25). Note from Matthew 11: 13-14, we see that "…the prophets and the law prophesied until John…" The Lord was speaking of John the Baptist. With the arrival of John as the forerunner of the Messiah, the Kingdom of Heaven became the issue and the center of focus. From the ministry of John the Baptist onward, the Day of the Lord is the great theme of the New Testament scriptures. Except for the interruption of the prophetic program represented by the Pauline epistles, the New Testament scripture concerns the Kingdom of Heaven being set up on the earth.

Revelation 1:10-11

"[10]I was in the Spirit on the Lord's day, and heard behind me a great voice, as of a trumpet, [11] Saying, I am Alpha and Omega, the first and the last: and, What thou seest, write in a book, and send *it* unto the seven churches which are in Asia; unto Ephesus, and unto Smyrna, and unto Pergamos, and unto Thyatira, and unto Sardis, and unto Philadelphia, and unto Laodicea." (Rev 1:10-11)

John was not physically translated through time to the future but he was in the spirit on the Day of the Lord (Rev. 4:1; 17:10; Ezek. 1:1; 11:1, 24). Isaiah 2:10 defines the Day of the Lord – The Lord alone shall be exalted on that day. Everything from here on in the book describes events that will transpire in the Day of the Lord.

Verse 10 speaks of the sound of a trumpet. The sound of a trumpet signals warfare. The Dispensation of Grace is over when this trumpet sounds.

The commentaries tell us that there is no historical record of a church there in Thyatira – therefore we might conclude that all of these could be future churches. However, there is much evidence that these churches were there in the Acts period. These churches are all in what we call Asia minor (or Turkey) today. In Acts 16:6 & 7, Paul was forbidden of the Holy Ghost to preach the word in Asia or Bithynia at that time. This is the only place where Paul was forbidden by the Holy Spirit to preach. We wonder why the Holy Ghost would forbid him to preach the word in Asia or anywhere for that matter. However, if God had these circumcision believers organized into Jewish churches, then we can understand that there was a reason for this. Peter wrote to Jewish believers in Asia (1Peter 1:1). James wrote to the twelve tribes scattered. It must be noted however, that the instruction that is given to these churches is the instruction that will be followed by the believing remnant of Israel in the coming tribulation period which (when followed) will get them through the tribulation and into the kingdom.

Christ the Son of Man, the First and the Last

Revelation 1:12-18

"¹²And I turned to see the voice that spake with me. And being turned, I saw seven golden candlesticks; ¹³ And in the midst of the seven candlesticks *one* like unto the Son of man, clothed with a garment down to the foot, and girt about the paps with a golden girdle. ¹⁴ His head and *his* hairs *were* white like wool, as white as snow; and his eyes *were* as a flame of fire; ¹⁵ And his feet like unto fine brass, as if they burned in a furnace; and his voice as the sound of many waters. ¹⁶ And he had in his right hand seven stars: and out of his mouth went a sharp twoedged sword: and his countenance *was* as the sun shineth in his strength. ¹⁷ And when I saw him, I fell at his feet as dead. And he laid his right hand upon me, saying unto me, Fear not; I am the first and the last: ¹⁸ I *am* he that liveth, and was dead; and, behold, I am alive for evermore, Amen; and have the keys of hell and of death." (Rev 1:12-18)

The term the Son of man is a title for the Lord Jesus Christ. It is a reference to Him as the king over all the earth. The first occurrence in the New Testament is in Matthew 8:20; the last is in Revelation 14:14. See also Daniel 7:13. In John 5:25-27 both titles "the Son of God" and "the Son of Man" is used. As the Son of God He has authority to give life, as the Son of Man He has authority to rule over men. The title that He had before He became a man was "The Word" (John 1:1-4, 14). He is called the Word because the volume of the Book – the Bible is about Him (Hebrews 10:7). His appearance with eyes as a flame of fire pictures one coming in fierce wrath. The brass speaks of judgment. The keys here represent authority over hell and death. He has authority to release people from death and to bind people with death.

John was to write what he saw

Revelation 1:19-20

"¹⁹Write the things which thou hast seen, and the things which are, and the things which shall be hereafter; ²⁰ The mystery of the seven stars which thou sawest in my right hand, and the seven golden candlesticks. The seven stars are the angels of the seven churches: and the seven candlesticks which thou sawest are the seven churches." (Rev 1:19&20)

John was to write:
- o The things (the signs) which thou hast seen – He was to record the vision (the whole book).
- o The things which are – He was to record what the things that he saw are (the interpretation of what they represent).
- o The things which shall be hereafter – by interpreting what he saw, he will be defining what the prophetic events depicted are (the events that will one day happen on earth).

He was to write "…the things which are…" what real world events they are (or in other words) what they represent. For example:
- o Revelation 1:20 "…the seven stars are the angels of the seven churches.
- o Revelation 4:5 "…seven lamps of fire …which are the seven Spirits of God. (Isa. 11:2)
- o Revelation 5:6 "…having seven horns and seven eyes which are the seven Spirits of God…"
- o Revelation 5:8 "…golden vials full of odors which are the prayers of the saints."
- o Revelation 7:13 "…what are these which are arrayed… these are they which are come out of the tribulation."

There are three things that I recommend that you bear in mind as you study the Book of the Revelation:
1. It is a record of future events that will occur in the Day of the Lord.
2. The book is self interpreting – what the things seen actually represent is explained in the Book.

3. The events in the book are in sequential and chronological order as they will occur in the Day of the Lord.

Note that there is a study available on DVD by Keith Blades that presents seven separate series of seven as all happening concurrently. He calls that approach "looping parallelism." Richard Jordan presented a series on the Revelation in which he sees the seven series being chronologically in sequence. In my opinion, the chronological approach seems to fit the flow of the events in a more logical fashion. This study therefore assumes that the series are occurring in chronological sequence. However, I welcome your thoughts on this.

The Letters to the Seven Churches in summary

Church	View of Christ	Problem to address	Solution to Problem	Situation	Promise to Overcommers	Challenge	Praise
Ephesus 2:1-7	7 Stars 7 Candlesticks	False Prophets	Repent Do the first works	They left their first love	Access to the Tree of Life	Remember and Repent	Laboring Faithfully. They hate the deeds of the Nicolatains
Smyrna 2:8-11	First and Last Was dead but now alive	Tribulation Poverty	False Jews to Synagogue of Satan	Satan will cast some into Prison Don't be afraid	Be faithful onto death I will give you a crown of life	Not hurt with the second death	
Pergamos 2:12-17	Has two edged Sword	Dwell where Satan's seat is	Repent	Antipas was killed there Some have doctrine of Balaam	Will eat the hidden manna I will give a white stone I will give a New Name	White stone and a New name	You hold forth my name and are faithful
Thyatira 2:18-29	Son of God Eyes as Fire Feet as Brass	Puts up with Jezebel	Repent or Great Tribulation	False Prophets teach servants to commit fornication	Power over the nations Will rule with a rod of iron Will be given the morning star	Will give to everyone according to their works. Hold fast until Jesus comes	Charity, Service, Faith, Patience, works
Sardis 3:1-6	7 Spirits 7 Stars	Dead	Be watchful Stir up what is ready to die	You are dead	Clothed with white raiment Name not blotted out of the Book of Life Will confess his name onto the Father	Strengthen what remains	Some have not defiled their garments
Philadelphia 3:7-13	Holy / True Key of David Opens Shuts	False Jews	Jesus will make them to worship	An open door	Jesus will keep them from the hour of temptation. Pillar in the temple will carry the name of the city of God	Keep the word of Prophecy. Jesus will keep them from the hour of temptation.	Kept the Word and has not denied
Laodicea 3:14-22	The Amen Faithful/True Witness Beginning of the Creation of God	They don't know are wretched	Buy gold tried in a furnace	I Chasten those I love Therefore Repent	Open the door and I will come in	Don't be luke warm	You will sit with me on my throne

Revelation Chapter 1 Study Guide Questions

1. What is the subject of the Book of the Revelation?

2. What is the reader of Revelation admonished to do in verse 3?

3. What concept does the word "church" carry? What is so special about these 7 churches in Asia?

4. Why the three tenses in the greeting in verse 4?

5. What three offices of Christ are exemplified in verse 5?

6. Where was John when he wrote the Revelation (verse 7)? Why was he there?

7. How did John see the future events (verses 10 &11)? Was he transported through time and brought back?

8. What does Christ's title "The Son of Man" imply (verse 13)?

9. What (according to verse 19) was John to write?

CHAPTER 2

The things the Lord Jesus Christ tells John to write to the angel (minister) of the church in Ephesus.

In chapter 2 we begin to address the seven churches. We will notice that each message to each of the seven churches has something in common with each other message.

- Each starts the same way. Each message starts with how John saw the Lord in Chapter 1. In each it is said "I know your works…" (Rev. 2:2; 2:9; 2:13; 2:19; 3:1&2; 3:8; 3:15). These churches stand in a right relationship to God on the basis of works. We today in the dispensation of grace stand before God on the basis of grace (Eph. 2:8-10; Tit. 3:5). In God's program with Israel, works are a factor in soul salvation. We see this in James 2:24 in writing to the twelve tribes scattered abroad saying "Ye see then how that by works a man is justified, and not by faith only." James goes to an experience in the life of the circumcised Abraham in Genesis Chapter 22 to illustrate how he was justified by works in offering Isaac. The apostle Paul on the other hand goes to an experience in the life of the uncircumcised Abram to show that a man is justified by faith without works in Genesis 15:6. Paul states "Now to him that worketh is the reward not reckoned of grace, but of debt. But to him that worketh not, but believeth on him that justifieth the ungodly, his faith is counted for righteousness." (Romans 4:4-5) That contrast defies for us the basis difference between the gospel of the circumcision and the gospel of the uncircumcision (Gal. 2: 8-9). God took the law out of the way for us today in the dispensation of grace. That however was not the case in the gospel of the circumcision (Matt. 23:1-3 cf. Matt. 28:20).

- Each message is addressed to the angel of the church. (See Psa. 110:1 cf. Acts 2:35) But why are these letters written to the angels of the churches and not to the elders? The logical explanation is that the information is addressed to a future generation of Israelite. Hebrews. 1:13-14 – "Angels are ministering spirits sent to minister for them who shall be heirs of salvation" in Israel's program. The current (contemporary) human ministers will not be there when the information must be applied. Therefore, the messages are given to angels (messengers) who can convey the message to those who will administer it. The seven stars are the angels to the seven churches.

- Each message addresses a different problem that the tribulation saints will face (2:7, 11).

- Each gives a solution to the problem.

- Each message talks about overcoming tough situations that the circumcision churches will have to overcome in the tribulation period.

- Each ends with a promise to those that overcome the problem.

- Each ends with the challenge "He that hath an ear to hear let him hear what the Spirit says to the churches." (2:7; 2:11; 2:17; 2:29; 3:6; 3:13; 3:22). This is a challenge to hear what Christ has to say and then to obey what he tells them to do (cf. John 10:27-28).

- The promises presented in Chapters 2 and 3 refer to things that are recorded in Chapters 19, 20, 21, and 22.

- Each message is addressed to all of the churches ("…let him hear what the Spirit says to the churches…" See 1:4, 11, 20; 2:7, 11, 17, 23, 29; 3:6; 13:22; 22:16) The message to each is a message to all.

- There is a pattern to each message
  - The Lord Jesus Christ is watching over each church.
  - He knows their works.
  - He sees their problem.
  - He gives instructions on how to deal with the problem.
  - He emphasizes enduring.

To the angel of the church at Ephesus

Revelation 2:1

> "Unto the angel of the church of Ephesus write; These things saith he that holdeth the seven stars in his right hand, who walketh in the midst of the seven golden candlesticks;" (Rev 2:1)

Angels had a ministry to Israel in the Old Testament (2 Kings 6:13-20). Angels ministered to Israel during the Acts period while Messiah is absent from them (Heb. 1:13, 14). In Paul's epistles, that is not the case. In Paul's epistles, angels are seen as learning about the wisdom of God by observing the functioning of the Body of Christ under grace (Eph. 3:10).

There were two churches at Ephesus during the period covered during the early part of the Book of Acts. Paul wrote to the saints regarding their standing in grace (Eph. 1:1; 2:8-9) who were sealed with the Spirit (Eph. 1:13) while John wrote to the other whose standing depended upon works (Rev. 2:2) with promises to the overcomers (Rev. 2:7). These are local churches in both programs during the period of time covered by the Book of Acts.

Their works were Imperfect

Revelation 2:2

> "I know thy works, and thy labour, and thy patience, and how thou canst not bear them which are evil: and thou hast tried them which say they are apostles, and are not, and hast found them liars:" (Rev 2:2)

The tribulation saints will have to deal with imposters: false apostles (Rev. 2:2); false Jews (Rev.2:9); and false prophets (Rev. 16:13). An apostle is a specially sent one to a group of people. There will apparently be men claiming to be specially sent to the Tribulation saints but are imposters.

Patience will be an important quality in the life of the tribulation saints to get them through that time of trouble (Isa. 28:16; Heb. 6:10; 10:23; Rev. 13:4).

Their First Love

Revelation 2:3-4

> "And hast borne, and hast patience, and for my name's sake hast laboured, and hast not fainted. [4] Nevertheless I have *somewhat* against thee, because thou hast left thy first love."(Rev. 2: 3 & 4)

The term "…thy first love…" is a title for Christ to express His relationship to Israel. God chose Israel when nobody wanted her (Ezek. 16: 1-6). "…Thou art a holy people unto the Lord …not… because ye were more in number…but because the Lord loved thee…" (Duet 7:6-8). Yet Israel constantly rejected that love. Hosea's wife is an illustration of Israel's unfaithfulness to that relationship. Matthew 10:34-37 "He that loveth father and mother, son or daughter more than me is not worthy of me…" John speaks much of that love in his epistles (1John 2:15; 3:1, 10; 4:7, 17). To endure the tribulation, these people will have to love God and love each other. (James 2:5-8)

Their Candlestick Could be Removed

Revelation 2:5-6

"⁵Remember therefore from whence thou art fallen, and repent, and do the first works; or else I will come unto thee quickly, and will remove thy candlestick out of his place, except thou repent. ⁶But this thou hast, that thou hatest the deeds of the Nicolaitans, which I also hate." (Rev. 2: 5-6)

Here in verse 6 He talks about the deeds of the Nicolaitans. In verse 15 the apostle talks about the doctrine of the Nicolaitans. He says that He hates both their deeds and their doctrine. The Greek word for Nicolaitans is a combination of two words – one meaning "to conquer" and the other "the common people". This is something that has been going on since Genesis 11 beginning with Nimrod. There have always been religious, political, and economic systems that strive to conquer the common people. There are such systems today and they are effective. In this case (in the Revelation) it is "…those who say they are apostles and are not…" who are actually doing it. (Rev. 2:2) The true apostles do not operate that way (1Peter 5:3; 2Cor. 1:24). The tribulation saints will know who their apostles are (Matt, 19:28; 2Peter 2:1-2; 3:1-3). The tactic of the false apostles is to "…have men's persons in admiration because of advantage." (Jude 16). Their claim will be that Jesus Christ has not come in the flesh (1John 4:1-4). They do this to deny all that Jesus accomplished at His first advent to earth. They will seek to direct men to the antichrist as the messiah.

If you have an ear to hear, You need to Hear what the Spirit says

Revelation 2:7

"He that hath an ear, let him hear what the Spirit saith unto the churches; To him that overcometh will I give to eat of the tree of life, which is in the midst of the paradise of God." (Rev. 2:7)

It will be important for the tribulation saints to pay attention to what the Spirit says and to meet in churches (Heb. 10:25; Luke 4:16; Acts 15:21) as the overcomers. The expression "He that hath an ear to hear, let him hear…" is given as a solemn warning to pay attention to what is said.

To the angel of the church in Smyrna

Revelation 2:8-11

"⁸And unto the angel of the church in Smyrna write; These things saith the first and the last, which was dead, and is alive; ⁹I know thy works, and tribulation, and poverty, (but thou art rich) and *I know* the blasphemy of them which say they are Jews, and are not, but *are* the synagogue of Satan. ¹⁰Fear none of those things which thou shalt suffer: behold, the devil shall cast *some* of you into prison, that ye may be tried; and ye shall have tribulation ten days: be thou faithful unto death, and I will give thee a crown of life. ¹¹He that hath an ear, let him hear what the Spirit saith unto the churches; He that overcometh shall not be hurt of the second death." (Rev 2:8-11)

The name Smyrna means mryh - used in embalming.
- o Verse 8 is the description of Christ from Chapter 1 "…saith the first and the last, which was dead, and is alive…"
- o "I know thy poverty…" In Revelation 13:17 we see that they can not buy or sell unless they have the mark of the beast. The believers in the Tribulation period will be in poverty.
- o The reference to the synagogue of Satan means that there will be a false religious system devised by Satan that is built on a rock but not on Christ the Rock (Duet. 32:15-16, 31).
- o Verse 10 speaks of a 10 day period of testing. It could be that the devil through the antichrist will give to them a ten days ultimatum to decide to take the mark of the beast or face death.

Because Christ was dead but is now alive forever, the believer can be faithful unto death and be assured that he will also rise. Revelation 20:4 speaks of the souls of them that were beheaded for the witness of Jesus. The second death will not affect them (Rev. 20:4ff)

o   "He that hath an ear, let him hear what the Spirit saith unto the churches; He that overcometh shall not be hurt of the second death." (Rev. 2:11) is both a warning and a promise.

To the angel of the church in Pergamum

Revelation 2:12-13

"[12] And to the angel of the church in Pergamos write; These things saith he which hath the sharp sword with two edges; [13] I know thy works, and where thou dwellest, *even* where Satan's seat *is*: and thou holdest fast my name, and hast not denied my faith, even in those days wherein Antipas *was* my faithful martyr, who was slain among you, where Satan dwelleth." (Rev. 2:12-13)

The Word of God is sharper than a two edged sword (Heb. 4:12). It can be used for offence and for defense. It is also the sword of the Spiritand is a part of the armor that we carry today (Eph. 6:17).

Verse 12 refers to Satan's seat as being in Pergamos. Satan's seat apparently moves but will apparently be in Pergamum when the tribulation period starts or was there when Revelation was written. According to Ezekiel 28:12, it was once at Tyrus. Satan will always be on point to resist and to appose God's work.

Church history seems to know of no one called Antipas. Therefore he is probably a future person. The name means literally "against all". It would not be difficult to see where the world would regard a godly believer during the tribulation period as being against everything and everybody because of the great deception that will hold sway under the influence of the antichrist (2Thess. 2:10). There have been others in the Bible (at least eight) who had been named before they were born. Cyrus was one (Isa. 44:28 cf 2 Chr. 36:22).

The Doctrine of Balaam

Revelation 2:14

"But I have a few things against thee, because thou hast there them that hold the doctrine of Balaam, who taught Balac to cast a stumblingblock before the children of Israel, to eat things sacrificed unto idols, and to commit fornication." (Rev. 2:14)

The account of the story about Balaam is found in Numbers 22 and 23. Though the account in Numbers does not state so, this passage adds that Balaam, after failing to curse Israel, did teach Balak how to get God to curse Israel. (Numbers 31:16) Peter refers to him in 2Peter 2:14 -15 as an example of one who beguiles unstable souls. Paul mentions the results of his teaching in 1Corinthians 10:8. God will give His saints strength to resist such temptation (1Cor. 10:13) There will apparently be people during the tribulation period who will do the same thing as Balaam did for money. The fornication in view here is spiritual fornication – i.e. idolatry.

The Doctrine of the Nicolaitans

Revelation 2:15

"So hast thou also them that hold the doctrine of the Nicolaitans, which thing I hate." (Rev. 2:15)

There have not been people called or named "Nicolaitans" as far as church history is concerned. They too are apparently a future people. The name comes from a compound word consisting of "Nike" meaning "to conquer" and Liaos" meaning "the common people." The doctrine has been around for some time. That is what religion is all about – to control the common people. Such a religious system had been around during the Old Testament times (Judges 17:5- 10 cf Mat. 23:9). Jeremiah 44:15-17, 22 addresses this system as does 1Kings 19:18 and 2Kings 10:20-22. Revelation 17:5 identifies a religious system called "mystery Babylon the Great." We will address this system in more detail there in Chapter 17.

Repentance is Important

Revelation 2:16-17

[16] "Repent; or else I will come unto thee quickly, and will fight against them with the sword of my mouth. [17] He that hath an ear, let him hear what the Spirit saith unto the churches; To him that overcometh will I give to eat of the hidden manna, and will give him a white stone, and in the stone a new name written, which no man knoweth saving he that receiveth *it*." (Rev. 2:16-17)

The white stone is significant. It is white to symbolize the righteousness of the saints. A rock or a stone is associated with Jesus as Messiah and it likely represents authority. It therefore likely represents voting rights and positions of responsibility in the Kingdom. Peter's confession that Jesus is the Christ was the rock upon which the Lord will build His messianic church (Matt. 16:18).

To the angel of the church in Thyatira

Revelation 2:18-27

"[18]And unto the angel of the church in Thyatira write; These things saith the Son of God, who hath his eyes like unto a flame of fire, and his feet *are* like fine brass; [19] I know thy works, and charity, and service, and faith, and thy patience, and thy works; and the last *to be* more than the first. [20] Notwithstanding I have a few things against thee, because thou sufferest that woman Jezebel, which calleth herself a prophetess, to teach and to seduce my servants to commit fornication, and to eat things sacrificed unto idols. [21] And I gave her space to repent of her fornication; and she repented not. [22] Behold, I will cast her into a bed, and them that commit adultery with her into great tribulation, except they repent of their deeds. [23] And I will kill her children with death; and all the churches shall know that I am he which searcheth the reins and hearts: and I will give unto every one of you according to your works. [24] But unto you I say, and unto the rest in Thyatira, as many as have not this doctrine, and which have not known the depths of Satan, as they speak; I will put upon you none other burden. [25] But that which ye have *already* hold fast till I come. [26] And he that overcometh, and keepeth my works unto the end, to him will I give power over the nations: [27] And he shall rule them with a rod of iron; as the vessels of a potter shall they be broken to shivers: even as I received of my Father." (Rev 2:18 -27)

Works are referred to twice in verse 19. Works will be important for the Tribulation saints. Their works will be a required demonstration of their faith. Today in the dispensation of grace works are still important but the works today are the follow-up to salvation by grace through faith apart from works (Eph. 2:8-10).

Verse 20 speaks of Jezebel. Historically, Jezebel was the wife of Ahab and was the daughter of a priest of Baal. Likely, this is a reference to Baal worship which will again be prevalent in some form during the tribulation period. Idolatry here is spiritual fornication – taking worship that rightfully belongs to God and giving it to someone or something else. It is interesting that Baal is represented symbolically as a bull or ox. Comparing Ezekiel 1:10 with 10:14 we see that the face of a cherub is the face of an ox. Satan (Lucifer) is the anointed cherub (Ezek. 28:14). If the antichrist will come in his own name (John 5:43), then we understand that the antichrist will glorify Lucifer. This is interesting to think about. We can hardly think of anyone doing that today but it will be happening in the Tribulation period

Verse 24 talks about the depths of Satan. This is a reference to the depths of the depravity to which Satan has fallen. In Ezekiel 31:26 we see him taking comfort in the fact that other kings who had followed him (the antichrist) are tormented in hell with him. In Romans 1:24, 26, &28 we see the state of the Gentiles when they had been given up by God. The worst thing that God can do to a person is leave him to his own devises and to allow him to plunge to the depths of depravity. Once one starts to give vent and free reign to the indwelling sin nature, it starts to go deeper and deeper into its depraved nature.

Satan will make a seven year covenant with Israel (Dan. 9:27). This seven year long period covered by the covenant will comprise the tribulation period. Isaiah 28:14-18 refers to this covenant as a covenant with death.

Verse 26 speaks of the overcomers ruling over the nations. The government of the kingdom will consist of Israel as a re-gathered nation under the reign of David (Ezek. 37:20-28; Hos. 3:4ff). Under David will be the twelve apostles who will judge the twelve tribes of Israel (Matt. 19:28; Isa. 1:26). The twelve tribes will each reign over a twelfth part of the earth (Duet. 32:8ff).

Revelation 2:28-29

> "And I will give him the morning star. [29] He that hath an ear, let him hear what the Spirit saith unto the churches." (Rev 2:28&29)

Jesus Christ is the Morning Star (Rev. 2:28 cf. 22:16) and the Day Star (2Pet. 1:16ff). See also Job 38:7 where angels are referred to as "morning stars."

Revelation Chapter 2 Study Guide Questions

1. List some of the things that the messages to each of the churches have in common with each other.

2. Why was John instructed to write to the angels as we see in verse 1?

3. Who are the impostors of verse 2?

4. What is the first love of which verse 4 speaks?

5. What are the deeds of the Nicolaitions that the Lord hates? Do we see those deeds in the earth today?

6. What would cause the poverty of verse 9?

7. Where (according to verse 12) was Satan's seat located?

8. Who was Antipas of verse 13?

9. What is the doctrine of Balaam verse 14?

10. What is the doctrine of the Nicholaitans?

11. What is the significance of Jezebel in verse 20?

12. Who will rule with a rod of iron according to verse 27?

CHAPTER 3

The angel of the church in Sardis

Revelation 3:1-2

"¹And unto the angel of the church in Sardis write; These things saith he that hath the seven Spirits of God, and the seven stars; I know thy works, that thou hast a name that thou livest, and art dead. ²Be watchful, and strengthen the things which remain, that are ready to die: for I have not found thy works perfect before God." (Rev 3:1 & 2)

These people at Sardis are dead in the sense of Luke 15:24 with the prodigal son. In Israel's program, faith is made perfect by works (James 2:14-22). Works that are acceptable to God have to be generated by faith. We see from passages as in Matthew 25:34-40 that works are a part of salvation in Israel's program. Faith always expresses itself by obedience. Faith will always do what God asks it to do. In James, the experience of Abraham in Genesis 22:12 when he was willing to by faith offer up Isaac demonstrated his faith by his work. Abram was justified earlier when he simply believed God and it was counted to him for righteousness. That was in Genesis 15:1-6 when he simply believed a promise from God that he would have a son when he was beyond the age whereby he could have a son by natural means. Luke 8:4-18 illustrates the faith that an Israelite had to have to get saved in that program. Of the four types of people in that parable of the sower, only the last were saved. Israel had to have a faith that would endure to the end (of the tribulation) to be saved (cf. Matt. 10:22). Israel had a conditional security. "My sheep hear my voice and they follow me." (John 10:27) We today are justified by faith apart from works (Eph. 2:8-10 and Rom. 4:1-6). Israel is justified by faith that is demonstrated by works (James 2:24). Their faith is made perfect by works. Faith is the issue in both cases.

Revelation 3:3-6

"³Remember therefore how thou hast received and heard, and hold fast, and repent. If therefore thou shalt not watch, I will come on thee as a thief, and thou shalt not know what hour I will come upon thee. ⁴ Thou hast a few names even in Sardis which have not defiled their garments; and they shall walk with me in white: for they are worthy. ⁵ He that overcometh, the same shall be clothed in white raiment; and I will not blot out his name out of the book of life, but I will confess his name before my Father, and before his angels. ⁶ He that hath an ear, let him hear what the Spirit saith unto the churches." (Rev. 3:3-6)

This passage talks about not defiling their garments and being clothed in white garments. This is talking about a life of practical righteousness. This is the walk that is expected of the Circumcision believers. 1John 5:2-4 describes the faith that overcomes the world. It is a faith that keeps His commandments. Verse 5 talks about their having one's name in the Book of Life. The Book of Life is an interesting study in Scripture. See the notes at the end of this chapter for a study on the Book of Life. Verse 5 also talks about the Lord confessing their names before the Father. Matthew 10:32 says that they had to confess Christ before men to have Christ confess them before the Father.

To the angel of the church in Philadelphia

Revelation 3:7

"And to the angel of the church in Philadelphia write; These things saith he that is holy, he that is true, he that hath the key of David, he that openeth, and no man shutteth; and shutteth, and no man openeth;" (Rev. 3:7)

Here the Lord is presented as:

- He that is holy (Luke 1:35)
- He that is true (John 10:36)
- He who holds the key of David (Isa. 22:22)
- He who has the power to open and to close the Kingdom (Matt. 16:18 & 19; John 20:23). This is a reminder that for them that to enter the kingdom was to enter into eternal life and vice versa.

Dealing with False Jews

Revelation 3:8-9

"⁸I know thy works: behold, I have set before thee an open door, and no man can shut it: for thou hast a little strength, and hast kept my word, and hast not denied my name. ⁹ Behold, I will make them of the synagogue of Satan, which say they are Jews, and are not, but do lie; behold, I will make them to come and worship before thy feet, and to know that I have loved thee." (Rev. 3:8-9)

Works are important here as they are with us (Eph. 2:8-10) who live in the dispensation of grace. However, in the tribulation period, works are a required manifestation of the faith that justifies (James 2:24) while justification today is apart from works (Rom. 4:1-6). Today good works follow soul salvation as an expression of appreciation for the gift of eternal life. For the circumcision believers, works were an integral part of the soul salvation.

Here we wonder who these are that say they are Jews and are not. Gentiles could join themselves to Israel under the Law of Moses. Uriah the Hittite was a case in point. However these are probably those that converted to Judaism during the dispensation of grace when Israel was "...Not my people..." (Hosea 1:9) If Israel is not God's people during this time, then Israel has no authority to make converts that God would recognize. Proselytes to Israel's religion converted during the dispensation of grace when Israel was in their given up state (Rom. 11:11-15) would have no legitimate right to be called Israelites. It could be that these are the descendents of the people that converted to Judaism during this present dispensation. The Kazhar Jews might be a case in point.

There is a coming Hour of Temptation

Revelation 3:10

"Because thou hast kept the word of my patience, I also will keep thee from the hour of temptation, which shall come upon all the world, to try them that dwell upon the earth." (Rev. 3:10)

Verse 10 talks about patients as a fulfillment of Isaiah 28:16 "Therefore thus saith the Lord GOD, Behold, I lay in Zion for a foundation a stone, a tried stone, a precious corner *stone*, a sure foundation: he that believeth shall not make haste." The hour of temptation is what the Lord taught his disciples to pray for deliverance from in Matthew 6:13. This is referring to the time when Israel will be required by the antichrist to take the mark of the beast. Hebrews 10:36-37 "³⁶ For ye have need of patience, that, after ye have done the will of God, ye might receive the promise. ³⁷ For yet a little while, and he that shall come will come, and will not tarry."

Another Promise to the Overcomers

Revelation 3:11-13

"[11]Behold, I come quickly: hold that fast which thou hast, that no man take thy crown. [12] Him that overcometh will I make a pillar in the temple of my God, and he shall go no more out: and I will write upon him the name of my God, and the name of the city of my God, *which is* new Jerusalem, which cometh down out of heaven from my God: and *I will write upon him* my new name. [13] He that hath an ear, let him hear what the Spirit saith unto the churches". (Rev. 3:8-13)

The Lord tells His disciples that they will be hated of all men for His name's sake. (Matt. 10:22). Therefore we see the warning to hold fast their testimony. In verse 12 we find the first reference to the New Jerusalem. This is the city that Hebrews 13:14 spoke of: "For here we have no continuing city, but we seek one to come." The reference to crowns and a new name will appear again in Revelation19:12 but there the crowns will be on Christ and the new name on Christ. This is again the identifying of the tribulation saints with Christ.

To the angel of the church in Laodicea

Revelation 3:14

[14] "And unto the angel of the church of the Laodiceans write; These things saith the Amen, the faithful and true witness, the beginning of the creation of God;" (Rev. 3:14)

Jesus Christ is the beginning of the creation of God in that He is the one who started it – who began it. He is the end in that He is the one for whom it was created.

Don't be Lukewarm in Your Stand

Revelation 3:15-19

[15]"I know thy works, that thou art neither cold nor hot: I would thou wert cold or hot. [16] So then because thou art lukewarm, and neither cold nor hot, I will spue thee out of my mouth. [17] Because thou sayest, I am rich, and increased with goods, and have need of nothing; and knowest not that thou art wretched, and miserable, and poor, and blind, and naked: [18] I counsel thee to buy of me gold tried in the fire, that thou mayest be rich; and white raiment, that thou mayest be clothed, and *that* the shame of thy nakedness do not appear; and anoint thine eyes with eyesalve, that thou mayest see. [19] As many as I love, I rebuke and chasten: be zealous therefore, and repent." (Rev. 3:15 – 19).

This passage is talking about the chastening that Israel will be under in the Tribulation period. Hebrews 12:6 addresses this chastening that will come upon Israel during that time. This chastening will be the means by which God will purge out the unbeliever from the nation and will prepare the nation to receive her Messiah.

The Overcomers will Reign with Christ

Revelation 3: 20-21

[20] "Behold, I stand at the door, and knock: if any man hear my voice, and open the door, I will come in to him, and will sup with him, and he with me. [21] To him that overcometh will I grant to sit with me in my throne, even as I also overcame, and am set down with my Father in his throne. [22] He that hath an ear, let him hear what the Spirit saith unto the churches." (Rev. 3:20 & 21)

Verse 20 is an open invitation for people to open the door of their heart – to believe that Jesus Christ is the true Messiah of Israel and the only hope for the world.

Verse 21 takes us back to Luke 19:17-23 where we saw that those of Israel who were faithful will reign over cities on this earth in the Kingdom. This compares with what 2Timothy 2:10-12 says regarding us who live in the present dispensation of grace. In both cases those who are faithful will reign with Christ. We will reign in the heavens (2Cor. 5:1) while the overcomers of Israel will do so in the earth.

Notes on the Book of Life
>In Revelation 20:12 we see different kinds of books.
>1. The book of life.
>2. The books.

These two different kinds of books can be found throughout the Bible. Consider the following passages:

The Book of Israel's Covenant Blessing

Exodus 32: 32 "Yet now, if thou wilt forgive their sin--; and if not, blot me, I pray thee, out of thy book which thou hast written."

Psalm 56:8 "Thou tellest my wanderings: put thou my tears into thy bottle: *are they* not in thy book?"

Luke 10: 20 "Notwithstanding in this rejoice not, that the spirits are subject unto you; but rather rejoice, because your names are written in heaven."

Hebrews 12:22 & 23 "But ye are come unto mount Sion, and unto the city of the living God, the heavenly Jerusalem, and to an innumerable company of angels, To the general assembly and church of the firstborn, which are written in heaven, and to God the Judge of all, and to the spirits of just men made perfect,..."
Ezekiel 13:8 & 9 "Therefore thus saith the Lord GOD; Because ye have spoken vanity, and seen lies, therefore, behold, I *am* against you, saith the Lord GOD. And mine hand shall be upon the prophets that see vanity, and that divine lies: they shall not be in the assembly of my people, neither shall they be written in the writing of the house of Israel, neither shall they enter into the land of Israel; and ye shall know that I *am* the Lord GOD."

The Book of Life
There are a number of references to the book of life in the Bible. Some of them are:

Philippians 4:3 "And I intreat thee also, true yokefellow, help those women which laboured with me in the gospel, with Clement also, and *with* other my fellowlabourers, whose names *are* in the book of life."

Revelation 13:8 "And all that dwell upon the earth shall worship him, whose names are not written in the book of life of the Lamb slain from the foundation of the world."

Revelation 20:5 "And whosoever was not found written in the book of life was cast into the lake of fire." We clearly see from this passage that if your name is not in the Book of Life, you are headed for the lake of fire.

Revelation 21:27 "And there shall in no wise enter into it any thing that defileth, neither *whatsoever* worketh abomination, or *maketh* a lie: but they which are written in the Lamb's book of life." We see equally as well that those who are written in the Book of Life go into eternal life.

Now this brings up a question: "Did God decide before hand who would be saved and who wouldn't? In a quick answer: No! God desires that all men be saved and come to the knowledge of the truth (1Tim. 2:4). The invitation is always "whosoever will, may come." It is God's pleasure to save all who take Him up on the invitation.

1Corinthians 1:21 "For after that in the wisdom of God the world by wisdom knew not God, it pleased God by the foolishness of preaching to save them that believe." God in His sovereignty chose to save "…them that believe…" that in eternity they will "…be holy and without blame…"

Ephesians 1:4 "According as he hath chosen us in him before the foundation of the world, that we should be holy and without blame before him in love:" Note: it does not say "…to be in Him..." but rather "He chose us in Him" – this is a corporate choosing (election). God decided before the foundation of the world that He will call out the Body of Christ and choose that body of believers so that every member of it would be holy and without blame before him in love. He did not choose who will believe but He chooses those that do believe.

Revelation 22:19 "And if any man shall take away from the words of the book of this prophecy, God shall take away his part out of the book of life, and out of the holy city, and *from* the things which are written in this book." Notice that it does not say "…take away his name out of the Book of Life…" but it says "…take away his part…" There is a place where everyone's name could be written. The people in the tribulation period referred to here could have the place where their name could be written removed. That means they would have no chance of being saved. This is the unpardonable sin that passages as Matthew 12:31, Hebrews 6:4, and 1John 5:16 address.

The Book of Life is a list of the names of the elect. If you have trusted Jesus Christ as Savior, your name will not be taken out of the Book of Life. Passages that talk about removing names are talking about another book – the Book of Israel's national blessings under their covenants. The following are some of the passages that address these blessings. Israel will have to endure to enter these blessings.

Psalm 69:28 "Let them be blotted out of the book of the living, and not be written with the righteous."

Isaiah 4:3 "And it shall come to pass, *that he that is* left in Zion, and *he that* remaineth in Jerusalem, shall be called holy, *even* every one that is written among the living in Jerusalem:"

There is another book referenced in the Bible called the book of the Living. We will address that book in Chapter 20.

Revelation Chapter 3 Study Guide Questions

1. In what sense were the works in verse 2 imperfect?

2. What would happen to a person if his name were blotted out of the Book of Life as verse 5 suggests could happen?

3. Who are the false Jews in verse 9?

4. What is "the hour of temptation" that verse 10 talks about?

5. What is the New Jerusalem that verse 12 talks about?

6. In what sense is Jesus "the beginning of the creation of God" (vs 12)?

7. What is the Book of Life?

CHAPTER 4

A Visit to the Throne Room of God

The events in Revelation Chapters 4 and 5 all occur in heaven. The throne in Revelation 4 is the same one as in Revelation 3:21. It is the Father's throne. The Lord's throne is on the earth (or will be on the earth when the kingdom is set up). John saw the same thing that Ezekiel saw in Ezekiel Chapter 1. There are 24 elders in verse 4. Twelve is the number for government. We ask who theses are. We will see these 24 elders several times throughout the Book (Rev. 4:4, 10; 5:8, 14; 11:16; and 19:4). The Book of Revelation is about God reclaiming the earth for Himself. All things in heaven and earth are created by Jesus Christ and for Him (Col. 1:16; Rev. 10:6). Both arte today in the hands of usurper (Eph. 2:2, 2Cor. 4:4).What was accomplished by the cross will enable Him to reconcile all things back to Himself (Col. 1:20) whether they be in heaven or on earth. The reconciling of this verse is not the reconciling of the persons who currently occupy those positions but rather to reconcile saints who have trusted Jesus Christ as Savior who will then fill those positions once they are vacated of the present occupants. This might lead one to think that twelve of these represent the heavens and twelve represent the earth. However, the members of the church which is Christ's Body (the church of this present dispensation) will have bodies that are eternal in the heavens (2Cor. 5:1) and they will reign there in the heavens (2Tim. 2:12) where they will judge angels (1Cor. 6:3). These twenty four elders will reign on the earth (Rev. 5:8). Therefore we understand that they represent Israel. It is therefore more likely that they are the twelve patriarchs of Israel and the twelve apostles who will sit on twelve thrones judging the twelve tribes of Israel (Matt. 19:28).

Colossians Chapter 1 on the Reconciling of all things

Colossians 1:15-20

"^{15} Who is the image of the invisible God, the firstborn of every creature: ^{16} For by him were all things created, that are in heaven, and that are in earth, visible and invisible, whether *they be* thrones, or dominions, or principalities, or powers: all things were created by him, and for him: ^{17} And he is before all things, and by him all things consist. ^{18} And he is the head of the body, the church: who is the beginning, the firstborn from the dead; that in all *things* he might have the preeminence. ^{19} For it pleased *the Father* that in him should all fulness dwell; ^{20} And, having made peace through the blood of his cross, by him to reconcile all things unto himself; by him, *I say*, whether *they be* things in earth, or things in heaven." (Col 1:15-20)

One of the key pieces of information that we find revealed by Jesus through Paul is the reconciling of all things back to God. The all things include the things in heaven and the things in the earth. The elect agency through which God does that is different for these two locales. It is the church -- the body of Christ (the church of this present dispensation of grace) that that He uses to reconcile the heavenly places to Himself. It is the mystery program found in the Pauline epistles that lay out how that will play out in time. It is redeemed Israel however, that will be the elect agency that he will use to reconcile this earth to Himself. The books of Hebrews through the Revelation reveal the details of how He will do that.

John sees the throne of God in heaven

Revelation 4:1-7

" ^{1} After this I looked, and, behold, a door *was* opened in heaven: and the first voice which I heard *was* as it were of a trumpet talking with me; which said, Come up hither, and I will shew thee things which must be hereafter. ^{2} And immediately I was in the spirit: and, behold, a throne was set in heaven, and *one* sat on the throne. [3] And he that sat was to look upon like a jasper and a sardine stone: and *there was* a rainbow round about the throne, in sight like unto an emerald. [4] And round about the throne *were* four and twenty seats: and upon the seats I saw four and twenty elders sitting, clothed in white raiment; and they had on their heads crowns of gold. [5] And out of the throne proceeded lightnings and thunderings and voices: and *there were* seven lamps of fire burning before the throne, which are the seven Spirits of God. [6] And before the throne *there was* a sea of glass like unto crystal: and in the midst of the throne, and round about the throne, *were* four beasts full of eyes before and behind. [7] And the first beast *was* like a lion, and the second beast like a calf, and the third beast had a face as a man, and the fourth beast *was* like a flying eagle." (Rev. 4:1-7)

The throne in heaven sits on a sea of glass. The voice that that he heard was "as the sound of a trumpet." There will be a trumpet that sounds at the time of the rapture but this event is not the rapture. The rapture of the Church which is Christ's Body happened before the Seventieth Week of Daniel Chapter 9 started.

The voice is apparently the voice of Christ. The Lord is calling John to see things in heaven. His visions will alternate between heaven and earth during the course of the Book of the Revelation. In verse 2 we see that he was in the spirit. This does not necessarily mean that he was taken there bodily to heaven. He is, however, seeing in the spirit things that are real and things that will be real in the end times..

Job 37:18 speaks of the sky being strong as a molten looking glass. Job 38:30 speaks of the face of the deep being frozen. This is likely the deep of Genesis 1:2 that had been separated to make way (the open firmament of heaven) for the sun, moon and stars. The throne is in the sides of the north (Isa. 14:13; Psalm 48:2; cf. Psalm 75:6, 7). In Isaiah 14:13-14 we see that Lucifer aspired to sit on that throne. "[13] For thou hast said in thine heart, I will ascend into heaven, I will exalt my throne above the stars of God: I will sit also upon the mount of the congregation, in the sides of the north: [14] I will ascend above the heights of the clouds; I will be like the most High." (Isa. 14:13-14)

The beasts that John sees are cherubim. Ezekiel saw them as well (Ezek. 10:14). These cherubim are always (when we encounter them in scripture) seen associated with the throne of God in some way. Here we again see the 24 elders. We will see them again in Chapters 5, 11 and 19 and will learn more about them there.

Verse 5 speaks of the seven Spirits of God. See the note on Revelation 1:4 regarding these seven spirits.

The Four Beasts with Six Wings

Revelation 4:8-11

"And the four beasts had each of them six wings about *him*; and *they were* full of eyes within: and they rest not day and night, saying, Holy, holy, holy, Lord God Almighty, which was, and is, and is to come. [9] And when those beasts give glory and honour and thanks to him that sat on the throne, who liveth for ever and ever, [10] The four and twenty elders fall down before him that sat on the throne, and worship him that liveth for ever and ever, and cast their crowns before the throne, saying, [11] Thou art worthy, O Lord, to receive glory and honour and power: for thou hast created all things, and for thy pleasure they are and were created." (Rev. 4:8-11)

Here we have a description of the four living beasts that are associated with the throne of God. There are two types of such beasts: there are seraphim and cherubim both of whom are associated with the throne of God. These are what might be called angelic like creatures but they are not angels. When angels appear, they appear as men as for example "the man Gabriel" in Daniel 9:21. These seraphim are described in detail in such passages as Isaiah 6:2. The creatures in verse 8 that have six wings are referred to as seraphim. Of the six wings, it is said that two are used to cover their face, two are used to cover their feet and two are used for flight. The creatures that we find in passages as Ezekiel 1:5-25 and in Ezekiel 10 are called cherubim and they each have four wings and each four faces. Of the four wings of the cherubim, two are used to cover their body and two used to fly.

Comparing the four faces of the cherubim in Ezekiel 1:10 with the four faces in Ezekiel 10: 14 will find something interesting. The four faces in Chapter 1 are the face of a man, of an ox, of a lion, and of an eagle while in Chapter 10 the face of the ox is said to be the face of a cherub. What is interesting about this is that Lucifer is said to be "the anointed cherub that covereth…" (Ezekiel 28:14). So comparing the two descriptions of the cherubim in Ezekiel 1:10 and Ezekiel 10:14 we find that the face of a cherub is the face of an ox or a calf. This is interesting in that Baal is presented as a bull. Satan is a fifth cherub that is not present here. He was "the anointed cherub that covereth" (i.e. that covereth the throne). If that be the case, then we would understand that the worship of Baal would have been the worship of Lucifer himself. Interesting!

Revelation Chapter 4 Study Guide Questions

1. Where do the events of Chapter 4 take place?

2. John sees 24 elders seated around the throne. Who might these 24 elders be? Where will they reign?

3. What are the 7 lamps in verse 5?

4. There was a sea of glass like unto crystal before the throne in verse 6. What verses in Job 37 and 38 address this?

5. Who are the four beasts that we see in verse 8?

CHAPTER 5

The Book Sealed with Seven Seals

Chapter 5 introduces the seven sealed book. This seven sealed book is interesting. Jesus Christ takes this book from the Father. The book has seven seals. Whenever a seal is opened that antichrist appears on the scene. Whenever another seal is opened, another manifestation of the antichrist is revealed. The book is somehow connected with the right to the kingdom or perhaps more properly, the right to planet earth. Jesus Christ has the right to open the book. It is His right both by right of creation and also by right of redemption. However, whenever He opens a seal, the antichrist in effect challenges His right to it. It is interesting that when the children of Israel went into the land under Joshua, the land was divided into seven parts (Josh. 18:8ff) with each under a different nation (Acts 13:19). Each had to be expelled. What we are seeing in Chapter 5 here is what was described in Hebrews 12:18-22. "[18] For ye are not come unto the mount that might be touched, and that burned with fire, nor unto blackness, and darkness, and tempest, [19] And the sound of a trumpet, and the voice of words; which *voice* they that heard intreated that the word should not be spoken to them any more: [20] (For they could not endure that which was commanded, And if so much as a beast touch the mountain, it shall be stoned, or thrust through with a dart: [21] And so terrible was the sight, *that* Moses said, I exceedingly fear and quake:) [22] But ye are come unto mount Sion, and unto the city of the living God, the heavenly Jerusalem, and to an innumerable company of angels,…"

The Book of Revelation is about a kingdom set up on the earth that can not be shaken or moved (Hebrews 12:28 & 29). The Book of the Revelation will alternate between events in heaven and events in the earth. Jesus Christ is seated now in the heaven and will until The Father makes His enemies His footstool (Luke 19:11; Psalm 110:1). The events described here are described also in Daniel 7:9-14 where the ancient of days is the Father who gives to Christ dominion, and glory, and a kingdom, and that all people and languages should serve Him.

Revelation 5: 1-6

"[1] And I saw in the right hand of him that sat on the throne a book written within and on the backside, sealed with seven seals. [2] And I saw a strong angel proclaiming with a loud voice, Who is worthy to open the book, and to loose the seals thereof? [3] And no man in heaven, nor in earth, neither under the earth, was able to open the book, neither to look thereon. [4] And I wept much, because no man was found worthy to open and to read the book, neither to look thereon. [5] And one of the elders saith unto me, Weep not: behold, the Lion of the tribe of Juda, the Root of David, hath prevailed to open the book, and to loose the seven seals thereof. [6] And I beheld, and, lo, in the midst of the throne and of the four beasts, and in the midst of the elders, stood a Lamb as it had been slain, having seven horns and seven eyes, which are the seven Spirits of God sent forth into all the earth." (Rev. 5:1-6)

The seven Spirits of God are the characteristics of Christ. This is apparently also what the seven horns represent in Chapter 1 (see notes on Rev. 1:4b). These seven spirits are characteristics of Christ that is sent in the earth through believers. In every dispensation, God has a way to manifest His character and personality through His people. This will be much like how Christ lives in and through believers today (Gal. 2:20 and 1Tim. 3:16)

The Worthiness of the Lamb to Take and to Open the Book

Revelation 5: 7-10

"[7] And he came and took the book out of the right hand of him that sat upon the throne. [8] And when he had taken the book, the four beasts and four *and* twenty elders fell down before the Lamb, having every one of them harps, and golden vials full of odours, which are the prayers of saints. [9] And they sung a new song, saying, Thou art worthy to take the book, and to open the seals thereof: for thou wast slain, and hast redeemed us to God by thy blood out of every kindred, and tongue, and people, and nation; [10] And hast made us unto our God kings and priests: and we shall reign on the earth. " (Rev. 5:7-10)

The words in verses 9 and 10 are sung by the 24 elders. Peter writes to circumcision believers telling them they are "a royal priesthood, an holy nation, a peculiar people; that ye should show forth the praises on him who hath called you out of darkness..." (1 Peter 2:9). Here we see that the four beasts and the twenty four elders singing a song of redemption and singing about reigning on the earth. See the note on Revelation 4:4 regarding these elders.

The Seven Fold Worthiness of the Lamb

Revelation 5:11-14

"[11] And I beheld, and I heard the voice of many angels round about the throne and the beasts and the elders: and the number of them was ten thousand times ten thousand, and thousands of thousands; [12] Saying with a loud voice, Worthy is the Lamb that was slain to receive power, and riches, and wisdom, and strength, and honour, and glory, and blessing. [13] And every creature which is in heaven, and on the earth, and under the earth, and such as are in the sea, and all that are in them, heard I saying, Blessing, and honour, and glory, and power, *be* unto him that sitteth upon the throne, and unto the Lamb for ever and ever. [14] And the four beasts said, Amen. And the four *and* twenty elders fell down and worshipped him that liveth for ever and ever." (Rev. 5:11-14)

All things are created by Christ and for Christ (Eph. 3:9; Col 1:16; Rev. 10:6; Heb. 1:2-3; 2:10). All things are His by right of creation and all things are in the process of being reconciled back to him by right of redemption. It is on the cross of Calvary that Christ purchased redemption for people that will replace those that currently run heaven and earth.

In verse 12 are listed seven things the Lamb is worthy to receive. In verse 13 we see every creature (a creature being the living part of God's creation) saying: Blessing, Honour, Glory, and Power to Him that sitteth on the throne (God the Father) and to the Lamb (God the Son).

Revelation Chapter 5 Study Guide Questions

1. The Lamb in verse 6 had 7 horns and 7 eyes. What do these represent about Christ?

2. Why according to verse 9, is the Lamb worthy to take the 7 sealed books?

3. Who, according to verse 10, are to be kings and priests and to reign on earth? Who is this applied to by Peter in I Peter 2:9?

4. How many angels are referred to in verse 11? How many different creatures of God are referred to in this chapter?

5. Verse 12 lists 7 things that the Lamb is worthy to receive. List them.

CHAPTER 6

The Seventieth Week Starts

Chapter 6 of the Revelation begins the actual seventieth week of Daniel Chapter 9. The antichrist makes a covenant with Israel for one week. We read about that covenant in Daniel 9:27. When each of the first four seals is opened, a horse and rider emerges. The first is a white horse, the second is a red horse, the third is a black horse and the fourth a pale horse. In each case, the focus of the narrative is on the rider. In each case, the horse is different but the rider is apparently the same. Note, "…and he that sat on him…" is repeated each time. The rider on the white horse in Revelation 6 is the antichrist while the rider on the white horse in Revelation 19 is the Christ (Rev. 19:13). Satan is the great imitator of Christ. He wants to "…be like the most high…" (Isa. 14:14). A person must have an ear to hear (to hear the Word of God) to distinguish between them. Satan is a liar and the father of lies (John 8:44). He can transform himself as into angel of light (2Cor. 11:14) so as to appear to be the good guy. When he comes during the seventieth week he will bring strong delusion. Here he rides a white horse with a bow in his hand. Note that it is a bow without arrows because it is by peace that he destroys many (Dan. 8:25 cf. 11:21) as he comes in peaceably to take the kingdom by flatteries. Note too that Christ comes with a sharp sword which is the Word of God (Rev. 19:15). Both come to conquer. In both cases, death followed (Rev. 6:8; 19:14).

Four seals are opened, each followed in turn by a rider

Revelation 6:1-8

"¹ And I saw when the Lamb opened one of the seals, and I heard, as it were the noise of thunder, one of the four beasts saying, Come and see. ² And I saw, and behold a white horse: and he that sat on him had a bow; and a crown was given unto him: and he went forth conquering, and to conquer. ³ And when he had opened the second seal, I heard the second beast say, Come and see. ⁴ And there went out another horse *that was* red: and *power* was given to him that sat thereon to take peace from the earth, and that they should kill one another: and there was given unto him a great sword. ⁵ And when he had opened the third seal, I heard the third beast say, Come and see. And I beheld, and lo a black horse; and he that sat on him had a pair of balances in his hand. ⁶ And I heard a voice in the midst of the four beasts say, A measure of wheat for a penny, and three measures of barley for a penny; and *see* thou hurt not the oil and the wine. ⁷ And when he had opened the fourth seal, I heard the voice of the fourth beast say, Come and see. ⁸ And I looked, and behold a pale horse: and his name that sat on him was Death, and Hell followed with him. And power was given unto them over the fourth part of the earth, to kill with sword, and with hunger, and with death, and with the beasts of the earth." Rev. 6:1-8

Note that Death and Hell in verse 8 are capitalized meaning that they are proper nouns. These are names given to the rider of the fourth horse. This is the antichrist. He is death personified. This takes us back to a prophecy in Isaiah 28:15 - 18 "¹⁵Because ye have said, We have made a covenant with death, and with hell are we at agreement; when the overflowing scourge shall pass through, it shall not come unto us: for we have made lies our refuge, and under falsehood have we hid ourselves: ¹⁶ Therefore thus saith the Lord GOD, Behold, I lay in Zion for a foundation a stone, a tried stone, a precious corner *stone*, a sure foundation: he that believeth shall not make haste. ¹⁷ Judgment also will I lay to the line, and righteousness to the plummet: and the hail shall sweep away the refuge of lies, and the waters shall overflow the hiding place. ¹⁸And your covenant with death shall be disannulled, and your agreement with hell shall not stand; when the overflowing scourge shall pass through, then ye shall be trodden down by it." (Isa 28:15-18)

The covenant with death that verse 15 speaks of is the covenant tht the unbelieving nation of Israel makes with the antichrist. The nation at large will think that they are gaining his protection by this agreement.

Note from Revelation 6:8 that these will be serious and trying times for the earth. In three and one half years, one fourth of the earth's population could be destroyed by the sword, famine, and the beasts of the earth and with death. How will they kill people with death? Apparently this (death) is a particular way of dying. Each of the four horsemen represents a different manifestation of the antichrist.

The Fifth Seal – The Martyred Dead

Revelation 6:9-11

"⁹ And when he had opened the fifth seal, I saw under the altar the souls of them that were slain for the word of God, and for the testimony which they held: ¹⁰ And they cried with a loud voice, saying, How long, O Lord, holy and true, dost thou not judge and avenge our blood on them that dwell on the earth? ¹¹ And white robes were given unto every one of them; and it was said unto them, that they should rest yet for a little season, until their fellowservants also and their brethren, that should be killed as they *were*, should be fulfilled." (Rev. 6: 9-11)

There have been four seals broken so far. Consider what each of the seals reveal:

The first seal (verse 2) reveals the antichrist on a white horse with a bow and a crown to conquer.

The second seal (verses 3 and 4) reveals him, the antichrist on a red horse. He is given a great sword. He also has power to take peace from the earth.

The opening of the third seal (verses 5 and 6) revealed the antichrist on a black horse with a scale in his hand. This would speak of famine and rationing.

The opening of the fourth seal (verse 7) revealed him riding a pale horse with a career that resulted in one fourth of the earth's population being killed.

With the fifth seal, we see the souls of the martyrs asking how long before the Lord avenge their blood on them that dwell on the earth. They are instructed to rest a little season until the rest of their fellow servants should be killed as they were. This vengeance is seen in prophetic passages as Isaiah 2:11-23.

The fifth seal reveals the appeal of the martyred saints to God. The sixth seal starts the Lord's response to their appeal. Note from verse 9 that the souls were under the altar. This altar is in the heavenly Jerusalem and comprises the church of the first born (Heb. 12:22 & 23 cf. Exod. 4:22).They are souls in a disembodied state. These are the spirits of just men made perfect that Hebrews 4:22 talks about. They are made perfect by the New Covenant that the Book of Hebrews presents to Israel. The blood of the New Covenant was shed at Calvary (Matt. 26:28; Mark 14::24; Luke 22:20; 1Cor. 11:25). However, the inauguration of the New Covenant will not be made (implemented) until Jesus Christ returns to the nation at the close of the tribulation period (Hebrews 8:8, 13; 12:24)..

These souls referred to here do not include the souls of the members of the Church the Body of Christ. The "church which is His (Christ's) body will have been raptured (caught up) to heaven before the seventieth week begins. The eternal destiny of the church of this present dispensation of grace is in "…an house not made with hands, eternal in the heavens" (2Cor. 5:1). The house not made with hands is the resurrection body of each of the members of the church the Body of Christ. The souls under the altar that are in view here in Revelation 6:9 are going to be resurrected in the first resurrection of prophecy which we will see in Revelation 20:4-6. There are two resurrections referred to in the Book of the Revelation – the resurrection of the just referred to in Luke 24:14 is also called "the first resurrection" in Revelation 20:5. The resurrection of the rest of the dead (the resurrection of the lost of the ages) will happen after the thousand years expire. This second resurrection (i.e. of the rest of the dead) is what the Bible calls the resurrection of the unjust (Rev. 20:5, 11-15 cf Acts 24:15).

Now there is likely a question here as to why there is a resurrection of believers (the resurrection associated with the rapture) before the "first resurrection." The event that the apostle Paul talks about in 1Corinthians 15: 51 includes a resurrection ("the dead in Christ shall rise first…") but it includes more than a resurrection of dead saints of this present dispensation of grace. The rapture includes the catching away of believers who are still alive at that time ("Then we which are alive and remain shall be caught up together with them in the clouds, to meet the Lord in the air: and so shall we ever be with the Lord." – 2Thessalonians 4:15-17) We get our English word "rapture" for this event from the Latin "Rapto" translated by the words "caught up" in the Old Italic Bible. The two resurrections referred to in the Book of the Revelation are the two resurrections of the prophetic program. The resurrection associated with the rapture is a part of the mystery program that God revealed through Paul the apostle of the Gentiles. See the book "You and your Creator" by the same author on the events associated with the rapture.

The Sixth Seal – The Wrath of the Lamb

Revelation 6:12-17

"[12] And I beheld when he had opened the sixth seal, and, lo, there was a great earthquake; and the sun became black as sackcloth of hair, and the moon became as blood; [13] And the stars of heaven fell unto the earth, even as a fig tree casteth her untimely figs, when she is shaken of a mighty wind. [14] And the heaven departed as a scroll when it is rolled together; and every mountain and island were moved out of their places. [15] And the kings of the earth, and the great men, and the rich men, and the chief captains, and the mighty men, and every bondman, and every free man, hid themselves in the dens and in the rocks of the mountains; [16] And said to the mountains and rocks, Fall on us, and hide us from the face of him that sitteth on the throne, and from the wrath of the Lamb: [17] For the great day of his wrath is come; and who shall be able to stand?" (Rev 6:12-17)

The entire seventieth week of Daniel Chapter 9 is the "Day of His Wrath" but the wrath intensifies from Chapter 7 of the Revelation on (See the note on Isa. 2:10ff below) onward. The earthquake of verse 12 is found prophesied in Isaiah 2:19 "...when he arises to shake terribly the earth." The falling of the stars in verse 13 is likely a reference to a disturbance in the angelic heavenly realm that we see culminated in Revelation 12:7-9. Note from Revelation 1:20 we see that there is a connection between stars and angels. In Jude 1:6 we see that some angels are imprisoned under darkness – literally in chains of darkness. The darkness is the chain that binds them. Apparently angels need light in order to function and operate. The darkness renders them unable to do anything much like a prison would do to a man today.

The events in Revelation 6 occur in the first half of the seventieth week of Daniel 9. Daniel 9:26 implies that there is a gap between the end of the 69th week and the start of the 70th week. In that gap, Messiah would be cut off and Pentecost would occur. Also, the events of Revelation Chapter 1 through 5 occur in that gap. The letters to the seven churches are probably written in the early Acts period (about AD 47) but the fulfillment of the prophecies in them and the carrying out of the instruction in them will be done in the tribulation period. We know now that the entire dispensation of the grace of God also takes place in an interruption of the prophetic program that occurs between the end of the 69th week and the beginning of the seventieth week. The events of Revelation Chapter 6 through Chapter 19 all occur during the 70th week.

The seventieth week is divided into two parts. The first three and a half years are covered by chapter 6. Chapters 7 through 19 cover the second three and a half years. In Revelation 6:15, the mighty men of the earth try to hide themselves from Christ out of fear. When we get to Chapter 19, the mighty men of the earth are emboldened by the antichrist to think that they can successfully defeat Him (Christ). The Lord speaks of these two appearances that He will make in Matthew 26:64 and Mark 14:62. The first is when the people of the earth see him "...sitting on the right hand of power." The second will be when they see Him "...coming in the clouds of heaven." The first occurs in Revelation 6; the second in Revelation 19. Psalm 2:4 - 6 pictures these two appearances. "[4] He that sitteth in the heavens shall laugh: the Lord shall have them in derision. [5] Then shall he speak unto them in his wrath, and vex them in his sore displeasure. [6] Yet have I set my king upon my holy hill of Zion." (Psalm 2:4-6). God the Father had raised up Christ to sit on David's throne on the earth (Acts 2:31). In Acts 7:56 Stephan sees Christ standing at the right hand of the Father. This would signal that He was ready to make His enemies His footstool (Psalm 110:1; Matt. 22:44; Acts 2:35). However, instead, He saved Saul of Tarsus, revealed the mystery program through him, started forming the Church the Body of Christ, and sat back down to be the head of the church which is His body

(Eph. 4:8; 5:23). One day, he will call away the church to the heavens (1Thess. 3:13) which will be its eternal home (2Cor. 5:1) and then will return to the earth to show who is the rightful king of kings (1Tim. 6:14).

Note verse 12 "the sun became black as sackcloth of hair, and the moon became as blood;" The sun became as sackcloth…the moon became as blood… This is figurative language. The reference to the stars falling to the earth is also figurative. Obviously, if the stars (like our sun) fell to the earth, they would incinerate the earth with everything on it. This is the fulfillment of a number of Old Testament prophecies. By studying these passages, we can learn what this figurative language is communicating

> Ezekiel 32:7 "…I will cover the heaven, and make the stars thereof dark; I will cover the sun with a cloud, and the moon shall not give her light. 8 All the bright lights of heaven will I make dark over thee, and set darkness upon thy land, saith the Lord GOD."
> (Ezekiel 32:7-8).

> Isaiah 13:9-13 "9 Behold, the day of the LORD cometh, cruel both with wrath and fierce anger, to lay the land desolate: and he shall destroy the sinners thereof out of it. 10 For the stars of heaven and the constellations thereof shall not give their light: the sun shall be darkened in his going forth, and the moon shall not cause her light to shine. 11 And I will punish the world for *their* evil, and the wicked for their iniquity; and I will cause the arrogancy of the proud to cease, and will lay low the haughtiness of the terrible. 12 I will make a man more precious than fine gold; even a man than the golden wedge of Ophir. 13 Therefore I will shake the heavens, and the earth shall remove out of her place, in the wrath of the LORD of hosts, and in the day of his fierce anger."

> Amos 5:16-20 "16 Therefore the LORD, the God of hosts, the Lord, saith thus; Wailing *shall be* in all streets; and they shall say in all the highways, Alas! alas! and they shall call the husbandman to mourning, and such as are skilful of lamentation to wailing. 17 And in all vineyards *shall be* wailing: for I will pass through thee, saith the LORD. 18 Woe unto you that desire the day of the LORD! to what end *is* it for you? the day of the LORD *is* darkness, and not light. 19 As if a man did flee from a lion, and a bear met him; or went into the house, and leaned his hand on the wall, and a serpent bit him. 20 *Shall* not the day of the LORD *be* darkness, and not light? even very dark, and no brightness in it?"

> Zephaniah 1:14-16 "14 The great day of the LORD *is* near, *it is* near, and hasteth greatly, *even* the voice of the day of the LORD: the mighty man shall cry there bitterly. 15 That day *is* a day of wrath, a day of trouble and distress, a day of wasteness and desolation, a day of darkness and gloominess, a day of clouds and thick darkness, 16 A day of the trumpet and alarm against the fenced cities, and against the high towers."

> Also Matthew 24:29&30 "29 Immediately after the tribulation of those days shall the sun be darkened, and the moon shall not give her light, and the stars shall fall from heaven, and the powers of the heavens shall be shaken: 30 And then shall appear the sign of the Son of man in heaven: and then shall all the tribes of the earth mourn, and they shall see the Son of man coming in the clouds of heaven with power and great glory."

Note on Revelation 6:14: The heavens being rolled up as a scroll is again figurative language. It describes the opening of heaven to man's view. Note Job 26:9 "…He holdeth back the face of his throne." God has structured the current universe so that man can not look into heaven. Today, God requires that men approach him by faith but faith that is seen is not faith (Rom. 8:23-25; Heb. 11:6; 2Cor. 5:7). In the middle of the tribulation period though, the Lord will open up heaven to view from the earth. From this appearance of Christ until His appearance in Revelation 19, He is a warning to the people of the earth to repent. It is a testimony to the hardness of the unbelieving heart that in spite of such overwhelming evidence of Christ and who He is, the world still chooses the antichrist.

Job 26:5-14 "Dead *things* are formed from under the waters, and the inhabitants thereof. 6 Hell *is* naked before him, and destruction hath no covering. 7 He stretcheth out the north over the empty place, *and* hangeth the earth upon nothing. [Astronomers speak of a black hole in the northern sky with a bright light in the center of it.] 8 He bindeth up the waters in his thick clouds; [Gen 1:6] and the cloud is not rent under them. 9 He holdeth back the face of his throne, [Job 37:18] *and* spreadeth his cloud upon it. 10 He hath compassed the waters with bounds, until the day and night come to an end. 11 The pillars of heaven tremble and are astonished at his reproof. 12 He divideth the sea with his power, and by his understanding he smiteth through the proud. 13 By his spirit he hath garnished the heavens; his hand hath formed the crooked serpent. 14 Lo, these *are* parts of his ways: but how little a portion is heard of him? but the thunder of his power who can understand?"

Revelation 6 is a fulfillment of the prophecy of Isaiah 2:10ff.

"10 Enter into the rock, and hide thee in the dust, for fear of the LORD, and for the glory of his majesty.
- 11 The lofty looks of man shall be humbled,
- and the haughtiness of men shall be bowed down,
- and the LORD alone shall be exalted in that day.

12 For the day of the LORD of hosts *shall be*
- upon every *one that is* proud and lofty,
- and upon every *one that is* lifted up; and he shall be brought low:
- 13 And upon all the cedars of Lebanon [Assyria], *that are* high and lifted up,
- and upon all the oaks of Bashan [Persia],
- 14 And upon all the high mountains [kingdoms],
- and upon all the hills [seats of governments] *that are* lifted up,
- 15 And upon every high tower [military defense],
- and upon every fenced wall [fortifications],
- 16 And upon all the ships of Tarshish [the merchant marine],
- and upon all pleasant pictures [pornography].
- 17 And the loftiness of man shall be bowed down,
- and the haughtiness of men shall be made low:
- and the LORD alone shall be exalted in that day.
- 18 And the idols he shall utterly abolish.
- 19 And they shall go into the holes of the rocks, and into the caves of the earth, for fear of the LORD, and for the glory of his majesty, when he ariseth to shake terribly the earth.

20 In that day a man shall cast his idols of silver, and his idols of gold, which they made *each one* for himself to worship, to the moles and to the bats; 21 To go into the clefts of the rocks, and into the tops of the ragged rocks, for fear of the LORD, and for the glory of his majesty, when he ariseth to shake terribly the earth.

22 Cease ye from man, whose breath *is* in his nostrils: for wherein is he to be accounted of?" (Isaiah 2:10-22)

There are some interesting contrasts between Christ and the antichrist as can be seen in the following table of comparison.

Christ	The antichrist
Christ came down from heaven (John 6:38)	The beast ascends up from the bottomless pit (Rev. 11:7)
Christ comes in His Father's name (John 5:43)	Antichrist comes in his own name (John 5:43)
Christ is despised when He comes (Isa. 53:3)	Antichrist is worshipped and adored when he comes. (Rev. 13:4)
In the end, Christ is exalted (Phil. 2:9-11)	In the end, antichrist is cast down to hell (Isa. 14:9)
Christ came to seek and to save the lost (Luke 19:10)	Antichrist comes to destroy (John 10:10)
Christ is the mystery of godliness (1Tim. 3:16)	Antichrist is the mystery of iniquity (2 Thess. 2:7)
Christ is God's truth (John 14:6)	Antichrist is the lie (2Thess 2:11)
Christ is life (John 1:4)	Antichrist is death personified (Isa. 28:15,18

There are also some interesting similarities in that Satan's methods are to imitate God. Note the comparison:

Christ as an angel of God (Gal 4:14)	Satan is transformed into an angel of light (2Cor 11:15)
Jesus is called the Lord's Christ (Acts 4:26 cf Psa. 2:1&2)	Satan is an anointed cherub (Ezek. 28:14)
Christ is a Prince (Acts 3:15)	Satan is a Prince (Dan 9:26; Mat 9:34; 12:24; John 12:31; 14:30; 16:11)
Christ is described as a lion (Rev. 5:5)	Satan is described as a lion (1Pet. 5:8)
Christ seals His people (Rev. 7:3)	Satan marks his people (Rev. 13:16)
Christ has ministers (Rom. 15:16; 1Cor. 4:1; 2Cor. 11:23)	Satan has ministers (2Cor. 11:15)
Christ was raised from the dead (1Cor. 15:1-4)	Antichrist has a deadly wound that was healed (Rev. 13:7,8)
Christ went to hell (Hades) and came back (Acts 2:27)	Antichrist goes to the bottomless pit and comes back out (Rev. 11:7&8; 20:2,7)
Christ is the way (John 14:6)	Satan has a broad way (Matt. 7:13)
Christ is the rock (1Cor. 10:4)	Satan is a rock (Duet. 32:15,30)
Christ is the true shepherd (John 10:10)	Antichrist is the idol shepherd (Zech. 11:17)
Christ has a throne of glory (Matt. 19:28; 25:31)	Satan has a throne (Isa. 13:13)

Chapter 6 closes with a question "For the great day of his wrath is come and who shall be able to stand?" Chapter 7 answers that question. Chapter 7 is a parenthesis between the 6th and 7th seal. The appearing of the Lord Jesus Christ in Revelation 6:16 is foretold in Luke 17:24 "For as the lightning, that lighteneth out of the one *part* under heaven, shineth unto the other *part* under heaven; so shall also the Son of man be in his day." In Luke 17:26-30 the Lord draws a parallel between the days of Noah and the days of the destruction of Sodom with the day of the Lord. As we read Revelation 6:16 we see that idolatry is the issue that the Lord is finally addressing in the tribulation. Read Isaiah 40: 18 through 31 on the futility of idolatry. In Revelation 7 we find that there are two groups of people that will be able to stand in that day. There will be the 144,000 and there will be the multitude who stand against the idolatry of the antichrist (the idol Shepard of Zechariah 11:7).

Revelation Chapter 6 Study Guide Questions

1. Who is the rider on the white horse in Revelation 6:2? Who rides the white horse in Revelation 19:13?

2. Why are the words Death and Hell capitalized in verse 8? Who is this?

3. Daniel 9:27 and Isaiah 28:15 both makes reverence to a covenant. Who are the parties to that covenant? Why is it called a covenant with Death?

4. Where do the events of the first five chapters of the Revelation take place?

5. Where does the actual 7 year Tribulation Period start in the Book of the Revelation?

6. Give a one sentence description of the event revealed in each of the first six seals.

7. Can you identify another place in scripture where the great earthly work spoken of in verse 12 was prophesied?

8. Matthew 26:24 and Mark 14:62 talk about two separate appearances of Jesus. Where do each of these happen in the Book of the Revelation?

9. Revelation 6:12 uses figurative language of the sun, the moon and the stars. What does the figurative language refer to?

10. Revelation 6:14 is also figurative language. What future event is this describing? Matthew 24: 29 & 30 will help you answer this.

11. Revelation 6:17 raises a question: "...who shall be able to stand?" In Revelation 7 we will see two groups that will be able to. Who are they?

CHAPTER 7

The Mark of the Servants of God

Four Angels Temporarily Stop the Hydrologic Cycle

Revelation 7:1-3

"¹ And after these things I saw four angels standing on the four corners of the earth, holding the four winds of the earth, that the wind should not blow on the earth, nor on the sea, nor on any tree. ² And I saw another angel ascending from the east, having the seal of the living God: and he cried with a loud voice to the four angels, to whom it was given to hurt the earth and the sea ³ Saying, Hurt not the earth, neither the sea, nor the trees, till we have sealed the servants of our God in their foreheads." (Rev. 7:1-3)

These four angels will temporarily stop the hydrologic cycle that waters the earth. This is what causes the famine that is seen during the tribulation period (in Rev. 11:6 the two witnesses shut up heaven that it rain not). They will have the power of Elijah (James 5:17) to effect the weather.

This is a contrast between "the living God" as apposed to the idol (Duet. 5:26). Angels are prevalent through out the book of the Revelation. There is an interesting study of how angels ministered to Israel (Heb. 1:13; Psalm 91:5, 11; Psalm 34:7; 1Kings 19:5, 16; 2Kings 19:35; Luke 16:19; Matt. 13:36ff; 25:31; etc.). Angels (at least the elect angels) today however are not interacting with the saints among men but rather are watching what happens in the earth as God saves people by grace to form the church which is Christ's body (1Tim. 5:21; 1Cor. 2:7) and are learning about the wisdom of God as they do.

In Revelation 14:1 we will see that the seal is the Father's name. This (Rev. 7:3) is not the first time that the faithful of Israel were sealed to prevent their destruction with the wicked (Ezek. 9:4-11). Just as in Ezekiel's time with the judgment of the captivity, the judgment in the tribulation was to begin at the house of God (1Peter 4:17-19 cf. Ezek. 9:6)

144,000 Sealed Jewish Preachers

Revelation 7:4-10

"⁴ And I heard the number of them which were sealed: *and there were* sealed an hundred *and* forty *and* four thousand of all the tribes of the children of Israel. ⁵ Of the tribe of Juda *were* sealed twelve thousand. Of the tribe of Reuben *were* sealed twelve thousand. Of the tribe of Gad *were* sealed twelve thousand. ⁶ Of the tribe of Aser *were* sealed twelve thousand. Of the tribe of Nepthalim *were* sealed twelve thousand. Of the tribe of Manasses *were* sealed twelve thousand. ⁷ Of the tribe of Simeon *were* sealed twelve thousand. Of the tribe of Levi *were* sealed twelve thousand. Of the tribe of Issachar *were* sealed twelve thousand. ⁸ Of the tribe of Zabulon *were* sealed twelve thousand. Of the tribe of Joseph *were* sealed twelve thousand. Of the tribe of Benjamin *were* sealed twelve thousand. ⁹ After this I beheld, and, lo, a great multitude, which no man could number, of all nations, and kindreds, and people, and tongues, stood before the throne, and before the Lamb, clothed with white robes, and palms in their hands; ¹⁰ And cried with a loud voice, saying, Salvation to our God which sitteth upon the throne, and unto the Lamb." (Rev. 7:4-10)

We note that there are twelve tribes of Israel listed but the tribe of Dan is conspicuous by its absence. Perhaps the reason for this stems from that tribe's tendency for idolatry as we see it in Judges Chapter 18.

Verse 9 refers to palm branches being in their hands. Palm branches are associated with the feast of Tabernacles (Lev. 23:40). The feast of Tabernacles is the last of the seven feasts that God gave to Israel to commemorate annually. Israel lived out their prophetic future through their system of feasts every year. The Book of the Revelation closes saying that the tabernacle of God is with men (Rev. 21:3). Here in the Revelation, Israel's prophetic future is coming to reality. The 144,000 are the first that are called out of the nation. They will be the ones reaching the rest of the believing remnant. During the tribulation Israel will be scattered (Luke 21:20-23). In Acts 2:11 there were devout Jews out of every nation in Jerusalem for the feast of Pentecost. The great multitude that we see in this passage is further identified in verse 14 (quoted below) as those that come out of great tribulation. There will also be Gentiles saved during the tribulation (Isa. 49:5-10; Psalm 67)

The Vision of those who come out of the Tribulation

Revelation 7:11-15

> "11 And all the angels stood round about the throne, and *about* the elders and the four beasts, and fell before the throne on their faces, and worshipped God, 12 Saying, Amen: Blessing, and glory, and wisdom, and thanksgiving, and honour, and power, and might, *be* unto our God for ever and ever. Amen. 13 And one of the elders answered, saying unto me, What are these which are arrayed in white robes? and whence came they? 14 And I said unto him, Sir, thou knowest. And he said to me, These are they which came out of great tribulation, and have washed their robes, and made them white in the blood of the Lamb. 15 Therefore are they before the throne of God, and serve him day and night in his temple: and he that sitteth on the throne shall dwell among them." (Rev. 7:11-15)

The tribulation period covers the entire 70th week of Daniel Chapter 9. Remember that Chapter 6 covered the first half of the Tribulation. Verse 14 talks about the Great Tribulation. The great tribulation is the second half of the seventieth week (Matt. 25:15-21).

Verse 15 speaks of serving day and night in the temple. This is interesting in that there is no day or night in the New Jerusalem or in heaven (Rev. 21:5; 22:5). Therefore, this is apparently a reference to the millennial temple that is described in Ezekiel chapters 40 through 43. They will be kings and priests in the millennial temple (Rev. 1:6; 3:12; 5:10). We will see this again in the note on Revelation 21:18-21.

God will wipe away their Tears

Revelation 7:16-17

> "16 They shall hunger no more, neither thirst any more; neither shall the sun light on them, nor any heat. 17 For the Lamb which is in the midst of the throne shall feed them, and shall lead them unto living fountains of waters: and God shall wipe away all tears from their eyes." (Rev. 7:16-17)

Living in this sin cursed world that we live in today, one can only imagine what life on earth will be like in the kingdom reign of the Lord Jesus Christ.

Revelation Chapter 7 Study Guide Questions

1. What were the tasks assigned to the four angels in verse 1?

2. What were they to wait for in verse 3?

3. How many were sealed in verse 4?

4. Who were those in white robes in verse 13?

5. What is the difference between the Tribulation and the Great Tribulation?

CHAPTER 8

The Seventh Seal, Seven Angels Receive Seven Trumpets

Revelation 8:1

"¹ And when he had opened the seventh seal, there was silence in heaven about the space of half an hour." (Rev. 8:1)

What is the significance of the silence? It could be the expectation of what is in the seventh seal. There are passages that give us a clue to the scriptural significance to silence.

- "The LORD is good unto them that wait for him, to the soul that seeketh him. It is good that a man should both hope and quietly wait for the salvation of the LORD." (Lam. 3:25)
- "But the LORD is in his holy temple: let all the earth keep silent before him. (Hab. 2:20).
- "Hold thy peace at the presence of the Lord GOD: for the day of the LORD is at hand: for the LORD hath prepared a sacrifice, he hath bid his guests." (Zeph. 1:7)
- "Be silent, O all flesh, before the LORD: for he is raised up out of his holy habitation." (Zech. 2:13)

The Trumpet Judgments

Revelation 8:2

"² And I saw the seven angels which stood before God; and to them were given seven trumpets." (Rev. 8:2)

Trumpets are associated with war and judgment. (Jer. 4:19-29). They are also associated with Israel's feast of Trumpets. The Feast of Trumpets was a type of the re-gathering of the nation of Israel to the land. These trumpets however, signify the seven trumpet judgments on the earth. The seventh trumpet brings the statement "The kingdoms of this world are become the kingdoms of our Lord and of his Christ; and he shall reign for ever and ever." (Rev. 11:15). The seven trumpets lay out the Lord's work in reclaiming what is rightfully His by right of creation.

God Hears the Prayers of the Saints

Revelation 8:3-7

"³ And another angel came and stood at the altar, having a golden censer; and there was given unto him much incense, that he should offer *it* with the prayers of all saints upon the golden altar which was before the throne. ⁴ And the smoke of the incense, *which came* with the prayers of the saints, ascended up before God out of the angel's hand. ⁵ And the angel took the censer, and filled it with fire of the altar, and cast *it* into the earth: and there were voices, and thunderings, and lightnings, and an earthquake. ⁶ And the seven angels which had the seven trumpets prepared themselves to sound. ⁷ The first angel sounded, and there followed hail and fire mingled with blood, and they were cast upon the earth: and the third part of trees was burnt up, and all green grass was burnt up." (Rev. 8:3-7)

The first four trumpet judgments affect the inanimate creation. In the first, 1/3 of the trees are burned up. In the 2ⁿᵈ, 1/3 of the sea became blood and 1/3 of sea life died. In the third, 1/3 of the fresh water supply became polluted. The fourth resulted in the loss of 1/3 of the celestial light reaching the earth.

One Third of Sea Life Dies

Revelation 8:8-11

"'⁸ And the second angel sounded, and as it were a great mountain burning with fire was cast into the sea: and the third part of the sea became blood; ⁹ And the third part of the creatures which were in the sea, and had life, died; and the third part of the ships were destroyed. ¹⁰ And the third angel sounded, and there fell a great star from heaven, burning as it were a lamp, and it fell upon the third part of the rivers, and upon the fountains of waters; ¹¹ And the name of the star is called Wormwood: and the third part of the waters became wormwood; and many men died of the waters, because they were made bitter.' (Rev. 8:8-11)

This pollution of the fresh water supply of the earth gives us insight as to the purpose of the gift of the ability to drink any deadly thing and not be affected (Mark 16:16ff). Jeremiah 9:12-15 prophesies of this event. In Jeremiah 23:13-15 we see that the false prophets that promoted Baal worship were to be fed wormwood. There is a connection with Baal worship and the judgment of the wormwood.

The Three Woes

Revelation 8:12-13

"**12** And the fourth angel sounded, and the third part of the sun was smitten, and the third part of the moon, and the third part of the stars; so as the third part of them was darkened, and the day shone not for a third part of it, and the night likewise. [See Ezek. 32: 7-10]

13 And I beheld, and heard an angel flying through the midst of heaven, saying with a loud voice, Woe, woe, woe, to the inhabiters of the earth by reason of the other voices of the trumpet of the three angels, which are yet to sound!" (Rev. 8:12-13)

The last angel announces "woe, woe, woe" on the inhabitants on the earth because of the last three trumpets. In Luke 21:26 the Lord speaks of this time when men's hearts will fail for fear. These will affect not just inanimate things as the first four did but will affect people. Chapters 9, 10, and 11 deal with these last three trumpet judgments. Each of the last three trumpets brings a different woe on the earth. Each is associated with satanic and demonic activity.

- The fifth trumpet brings the first woe which releases demonic creatures from the bottomless pit. These will not kill men but will inflict pain on them and hurt people who did not have the seal of God (Rev. 9:4-10) for 5 months.
- The sixth trumpet brings the second woe releaseing four angels which had been bound in the river Euphrates. These angels lead an army of demonic horsemen 200 million strong which kill one third of mankind on earth (Rev. 9:15-19). This woe lasts one year, one month and one hour (a time period of 395 days plus one hour or 390 days plus one hour if the typical prophetic year is used).
- The seventh trumpet brings the third woe but we do not see that until Revelation 12:12. The third woe comes as a result of Satan being cast out of heaven and into the earth. This brings great tribulation to the people on the earth.

Revelation Chapter 8 Study Guide Questions

1. What is the significance of the silence in heaven in verse 1?

2. The seventh seal introduced the seven trumpet judgments. What do the seven trumpet judgments lay out?

3. What part of creation is affected by the first of four trumpet judgments?

4. What percent of the inanimate creation was affected by the first four trumpet judgments?

5. Revelation 8:11 presents the star wormwood which will poison 1/3 of the fresh water on earth. In Jeremiah 9:15 and 23:15 we see that the wormwood was directed at a certain false God. What false God was that? Does this give you any indication of what the religion of the anti-christ might be?

6. The fourth angel affected the sun, moon and stars. What was prophesied in Ezekiel 32:7-10 relative to this?

7. Each of the fifth, sixth, and seventh trumpets bring a woe. List the woe which each will bring.

CHAPTER 9

The Plague of Locusts Swarms Out of the Bottomless Pit

Revelation 9:1-2

"¹ And the fifth angel sounded, and I saw a star fall from heaven unto the earth: and to him was given the key of the bottomless pit. ² And he opened the bottomless pit; and there arose a smoke out of the pit, as the smoke of a great furnace; and the sun and the air were darkened by reason of the smoke of the pit." (Rev. 9:1 & 2)

The First Woe

The fifth trumpet brings the first woe (Rev. 9:13). The term "bottomless pit" referred to in verse 1 is translated from a word meaning literally "the abyss." The same word is translated "the deep" in Luke 8:31 "And they (the demons) besought him that he would not command them to go out into the deep." Studying the subject, we find that the abyss is a compartment in hell where demons are held. Satan himself will be held there during the millennium (Rev. 20:3).

There is a place called Tartarus (the Greek work translated Hell in 2Peter 2:4) where the angels that kept not there first estate (Genesis 6) are held. There are three different Greek words translated "hell" in our KJV. "Hell" is translated from "Hades" in Matthew 11:23; 16:18; Luke 10:15; 12:5; 16:23; Acts 2:27, 31. Hades had two compartments - Torments (Luke 16:23) where the lost are held pending resurrection and there is a compartment called Paradise (Luke 23:43) where the saved of the ages are held pending their resurrection to glory. However, Paradise is today in the third heaven (2Cor. 12:4; Heb. 12:23ff). It apparently had been moved to heaven after the death, burial, resurrection and ascension of the Lord Jesus Christ back to heaven.

"Hell" is translated from the Greek word "Gehenna" in Matthew 5:22, 29, 30; 10:28; 18:19; 23:15, 33; Mark 9:43, 45, 47; and James 3:6. Any reference to hell where both body and soul can be destroyed is a translation from the word Gehenna. Gehenna is actually a portal of entry into the compartment of Hades called "Torments." That portal of entry into Hades is described in Deuteronomy 32:22 and will be opened by the Lord Jesus Christ when He returns to set up His kingdom. That portal into Hades does not exist on earth today.

In Isaiah 66: 22-24 we see that Gehenna will be the means of capitol punishment in the Millennium. The physical location of Gehenna is given in Isaiah 34:1 ff. That area will be the habitation of some strange creatures which are apparently the degraded forms of fallen angels. Eventually, Hades, Tartarus, Gehenna, and the abyss will all be cast into the Lake of Fire (Rev. 19:20; 20:10, 14) which will be the ultimate place of disposal of all evil. Isaiah 34: 9 & 10 speaks of the dust being turned to brimstone and the land into burning pitch that shall not be quenched (referring to Gehenna).

Demons Released from the Abyss

Revelation 9:3

"³ And there came out of the smoke locusts upon the earth: and unto them was given power, as the scorpions of the earth have power." (Rev. 9:3)

These are not normal insects (Rev. 9:7). These insects according to Revelation 9:11 have a king over them named Abaddon in the Hebrew and Apollyon in the Greek. The names mean "destroyer" in either language. Normal insects do not have kings (Prov. 30:27).

The Demons Torment those not sealed by God

Revelation 9:4-12

> "4 And it was commanded them that they should not hurt the grass of the earth, neither any green thing, neither any tree; but only those men which have not the seal of God in their foreheads. 5 And to them it was given that they should not kill them, but that they should be tormented five months: and their torment *was* as the torment of a scorpion, when he striketh a man. 6 And in those days shall men seek death, and shall not find it; and shall desire to die, and death shall flee from them. 7 And the shapes of the locusts *were* like unto horses prepared unto battle; and on their heads *were* as it were crowns like gold, and their faces *were* as the faces of men. 8 And they had hair as the hair of women, and their teeth were as *the teeth* of lions. 9 And they had breastplates, as it were breastplates of iron; and the sound of their wings *was* as the sound of chariots of many horses running to battle. 10 And they had tails like unto scorpions, and there were stings in their tails: and their power *was* to hurt men five months. 11 And they had a king over them, *which is* the angel of the bottomless pit, whose name in the Hebrew tongue *is* Abaddon, but in the Greek tongue hath *his* name Apollyon. 12 One woe is past; *and*, behold, there come two woes more hereafter." (Rev. 9:4-12)

Also, aside from normal insects not having a king over them, normal insects would eat the grass and other vegetation. These go after men. The men that they go after to torment are those who do not have the seal of God. In Revelation 17:7 we see that the two witnesses will be killed by the beast that ascended out of the bottomless pit. The beast in Chapter 17 "…was and is not; and shall ascend out of the bottomless pit, and go into perdition…" (Rev. 17:8). It is interesting in verse 6 of this chapter that people will seek death in order to find relief from these insects but we will see in verse 20 that they will not seek repentance. This first woe upon men will last five months.

The sixth trumpet sounds

Revelation 9:13-14

> "13 And the sixth angel sounded, and I heard a voice from the four horns of the golden altar which is before God, 14 Saying to the sixth angel which had the trumpet, Loose the four angels which are bound in the great river Euphrates." (Rev. 9:13-14)

The 6th trumpet brings the second woe (Rev. 11:14). As we study the land mass that will be given to Israel in Genesis 15:18, the river Euphrates is at the eastern boundary of that land, the Promised Land. These are apparently fallen angels or else they would not be bound. They were apparently bound because their goal was to do what they do here – destroy the Promised Land or to keep Israel from possessing it. The Euphrates is the fourth of four rivers that split off from the river that ran out of Eden in Genesis 2:8-14. Genesis 15:18 describes the land that God promised to Abraham as being "…from the river of Egypt (i.e. the Nile) unto the great river, the river Euphrates." Deuteronomy 11:24 describes that land as being "…from the wilderness of Lebanon, from the river, the river Euphrates even unto the uttermost sea shall be your coast." Babylon is on the river Euphrates. In Revelation 16:12 we see a judgment upon the Euphrates to dry it up and make way for the invasion of the kings of the east during the sixth vial judgment.

That sixth vial also reveals the demonic spirits that deceive the kings of the earth to gather them to Armageddon. We will see more on this later. The ultimate destruction of Babylon is prophesied in Jeremiah 51:61-62. Revelation 18:21 records this ultimate destruction. Isaiah 13:19-22 also speaks of this final destruction.

The four angels are loosed to slay on third of the earth's population.

Revelation 9:15-19

"15 And the four angels were loosed, which were prepared for an hour, and a day, and a month, and a year, for to slay the third part of men. 16 And the number of the army of the horsemen *were* two hundred thousand thousand: and I heard the number of them. 17 And thus I saw the horses in the vision, and them that sat on them, having breastplates of fire, and of jacinth, and brimstone: and the heads of the horses *were* as the heads of lions; and out of their mouths issued fire and smoke and brimstone. 18 By these three was the third part of men killed, by the fire, and by the smoke, and by the brimstone, which issued out of their mouths. 19 For their power is in their mouth, and in their tails: for their tails *were* like unto serpents, and had heads, and with them they do hurt." (Rev. 9:15-19)

Verse 15 defines the time limit of the activity of the four angels – 391 days plus 1 hour. God limits the duration of each judgment or no flesh would be saved (see Matt. 24:22 on this). The events in the Book of the Revelation all tie into what we see prophesied in the four gospels. This in verse 16 is the army that is referenced in Luke 21:24 and this is the destruction of Jerusalem that is spoken of in Luke 21:20-24. See the note on this passage below.

Luke Chapter 21 talks about this time of trouble. The entire passage in Luke 21 the Lord is addressing the disciples' question "…when shall these things be? And what sign will there be when these things shall come to pass?" Luke 21:20-24 "20 And when ye shall see Jerusalem compassed with armies, then know that the desolation thereof is nigh. 21 Then let them which are in Judaea flee to the mountains; and let them which are in the midst of it depart out; and let not them that are in the countries enter thereinto. 22 For these be the days of vengeance, that all things which are written may be fulfilled. 23 But woe unto them that are with child, and to them that give suck, in those days! for there shall be great distress in the land, and wrath upon this people. 24 And they shall fall by the edge of the sword, and shall be led away captive into all nations: and Jerusalem shall be trodden down of the Gentiles, until the times of the Gentiles be fulfilled."

Remember that in Revelation 6:8 we saw that one fourth of the men of the earth were killed. In Revelation 8:11 many were killed by the wormwood. Here one third of the world population is killed. Combined, this would amount to over half of the earth's population that were on earth at the start of the tribulation period. These indeed will be hard times for those who dwell on planet earth. Verses 17 thru 19 describe creatures similar to what we see in 2Kings 2:11 where angels in chariots of fire took Elijah to heaven. However, these in Revelation 9: 15-19 are the fallen demonic version of the creatures in 2Kings.

Revelation 9:20-21

"20 And the rest of the men which were not killed by these plagues yet repented not of the works of their hands, that they should not worship devils, and idols of gold, and silver, and brass, and stone, and of wood: which neither can see, nor hear, nor walk: 21 Neither repented they of their murders, nor of their sorceries, nor of their fornication, nor of their thefts." (Rev 9:20-21)

"They repented not…" (Verses 20 and 21). There will be then (as there is today) a religious system that will keep people from repentance. Idolatrous religious systems do that today. The Lord dealt with such a system in His earthly ministry (Luke 16:29). In Romans 1:24 thru 28 we see that God gave them over to "uncleanness" and a "reprobate mind" because "…when they knew God, they glorified them not as God, neither were thankful; but became vain in their imagination, and their foolish heart was darkened." Yet today people are going back to monogamous marriages because of the AIDS and other STDs. However, here in Revelation 9, they will not repent even under the direct judgment of God. The reason for the judgment was idolatry (a blinding religious system of idolatry), murders (probably in connection with the practice of that religious system), sorceries (drugs, alcohol, witchcraft, etc), and thefts.

Isaiah 26:1-21 is a song that will be sung in the day that judgment is coming to the earth in the tribulation. Verse 10 of Isaiah 26 "Let favour be shewed to the wicked, *yet* will he not learn righteousness: in the land of uprightness will he deal unjustly, and will not behold the majesty of the LORD." This passage is instructive on Revelation 9 where men will not repent under grace.

Isaiah 26:8-11 "8 Yea, in the way of thy judgments, O LORD, have we waited for thee; the desire of *our* soul *is* to thy name, and to the remembrance of thee. 9 With my soul have I desired thee in the night; yea, with my spirit within me will I seek thee early: for when thy judgments *are* in the earth, the inhabitants of the world will learn righteousness. 10 Let favour be shewed to the wicked, *yet* will he not learn righteousness: in the land of uprightness will he deal unjustly, and will not behold the majesty of the LORD. 11 LORD, *when* thy hand is lifted up, they will not see: *but* they shall see, and be ashamed for *their* envy at the people; yea, the fire of thine enemies shall devour them." (Isa. 26:8-11)

It is an important thing to remember that sin hardens the heart. The hardened heart then becomes insensitive to the dealings of the Lord in the heart.

Revelation Chapter 9 Study Guide Questions

1. What or who is the star in verse 1 (we note that it is said of the star that "…to him was given the keys to the bottomless pit")?

2. What is the bottomless pit in verse 2?

3. Verse 11 tells us that the locusts in verse 3 had a king over them. What does this tell us about the locusts?

6. Are the four angels that were bound in the River Euphrates good guys or bad? What was their goal according to verse 15?

7. According to verse 18, which portion of humanity were killed by the horsemen?

8. According to verse 16, how many horsemen were there?

9. Where in Luke's gospel do we read about this army that will destroy Jerusalem?

10. According to verse 20, did the torments by the demon army bring men to repentance?

CHAPTER 10

John sees an angel with a book, and hears things he is forbidden to write

Revelation 10:1

"¹ And I saw another mighty angel come down from heaven, clothed with a cloud: and a rainbow *was* upon his head, and his face *was* as it were the sun, and his feet as pillars of fire:" (Rev. 10:1)

This "another angel" is not the angel with the sixth trumpet. This angel (the seventh) begins to sound his trumpet (10:7) and continues to sound his trumpet until the second woe is past (Rev. 11:13). Revelation10:1 through 11:12 is a parenthesis between the sixth and the seventh trumpet. Many believe that this angel is Jesus Christ. For sure, he represents Christ. Note some evidence to that effect:

- "A rainbow was upon his head…" In Revelation 4:3 John saw "a rainbow about the throne." The rainbow is a sign of the faithfulness of God (Gen. 9:13)
- His face was as the sun. Christ appeared to Paul as the brightness of the noonday sun (Acts 26:13).
- His feet as pillars of fire – sign of judgment. The Lord is coming to judge.
- Paul uses a picture of the possibility of Christ appearing as an angel (Gal. 4:14).
- His voice is as a lion. Christ is the Lion of the tribe of Judah (Rev. 5:5 cf Joel 3:16).
- He has an open book in His hand. Christ just opened the seven sealed book (Rev. 5:1-5). The seven seals are seven judgments that lead to the Lord taking repossession of the earth. Remember that He is the only one qualified to do so (Rev. 5:4-8).
- He has one foot on the sea and the other on the earth and a hand up to heaven. This is a jester of taking possession (Deut. 11:24; Joshua 1:3) of the sea, the land and the heaven. Christ is the creator of heaven and earth (Col. 1:16). There is a usurper who holds both today (Ephesians 2:2 and 2Corinthians 4:3-4). He will reconcile both back to Himself (Col. 1:20) by His redeeming work.

The Seven Thunders

Revelation 10:2-4

"² And he had in his hand a little book open: and he set his right foot upon the sea, and *his* left *foot* on the earth, ³ And cried with a loud voice, as *when* a lion roareth: and when he had cried, seven thunders uttered their voices. ⁴ And when the seven thunders had uttered their voices, I was about to write: and I heard a voice from heaven saying unto me, Seal up those things which the seven thunders uttered, and write them not." (Rev. 10:2-4)

The reference to the seven thunders takes us to Psalm 29:3ff where we see thunder from God associated with the voice of the LORD and with the number seven.

"³ The voice of the LORD *is* upon the waters: the God of glory thundereth: the LORD *is* upon many waters.
⁴ The voice of the LORD *is* powerful;
the voice of the LORD *is* full of majesty.
⁵ The voice of the LORD breaketh the cedars; yea, the LORD breaketh the cedars of Lebanon. ⁶ He maketh them also to skip like a calf; Lebanon and Sirion like a young unicorn.
⁷ The voice of the LORD divideth the flames of fire.
⁸ The voice of the LORD shaketh the wilderness; the LORD shaketh the wilderness of Kadesh.
⁹ The voice of the LORD maketh the hinds to calve, and discovereth the forests: and in his temple doth every one speak of *his* glory.
¹⁰ The LORD sitteth upon the flood; yea, the LORD sitteth King for ever.

¹¹ The LORD will give strength unto his people; the LORD will bless his people with peace. Psalms 29:3-11 lists seven things associated with the voice of the LORD."

The seven thunders appear to be associated with the coming seven vial judgments. The thunders are the voice of God associated with those judgments. In Revelation 10:4 John was told not to write what the thunders said. However, before the Book of Revelation is over, what the thunders said will have been revealed. Unlike the book of Daniel (Dan. 12:3-9) in which the words are closed up and sealed until the time of the end, the book of the Revelation is an unsealed book (Rev. 22:10). It is just that there is a delay in revealing what the thunders said.

The Times of the Gentiles is up

Revelation 10:5-7

"5 And the angel which I saw stand upon the sea and upon the earth lifted up his hand to heaven, 6 And sware by him that liveth for ever and ever, who created heaven, and the things that therein are, and the earth, and the things that therein are, and the sea, and the things which are therein, that there should be time no longer: 7 But in the days of the voice of the seventh angel, when he shall begin to sound, the mystery of God should be finished, as he hath declared to his servants the prophets." (Rev. 10:5-7)

"There should be time no longer..." means simply "Times up." The delay in God's judgment of the earth is come to an end. The world's rebellion against God is over (cf. Rev. 11:15).

The seventh trumpet needs to be addressed in that some people consider this to be the last trump of 1Corinthians 15:51. If that were the case, then the church the Body of Christ would being going through the first half of the tribulation period. Let's consider that possibility:

- The trump of 1Corinthians 15:52 happens in the twinkling of an eye. The trumpet of the seventh angel sounds over an extended period of time. (Rev. 10:7). In 10:7 the Seventh Angel begins to sound. In 11:15 the Seventh Angel sounded. Note that verse 7 speaks of "… the days of the voice of the seventh angel." The seventh trumpet here in Revelation 10 sounds over an extended numbers of days.
- The mystery of God in Revelation 10:7 hath been "…declared to his servants the prophets." The mystery of 1Corinthians 15:52 is something the prophets of the Old Testament knew nothing about.
- The trumpet of the seventh angel (Rev. 7) is not the last trumpet to sound. The Lord speaks of a trumpet that will sound after the seventh angel. In Matthew 24:31 the Lord speaks of the re-gathering of Israel saying "'And he shall send his angels with a great sound of a trumpet, and they shall gather together his elect from the four winds, from one end of heaven to the other." Matthew 24:31. This is the re-gathering prophesied in Isaiah 27:12 & 13.

Verse 6 is a reference to Jesus who is the creator of everything in Heaven and in Earth (Col. 1:16; John 1:1-4; Heb. 1:10-12). Verse 7 says that the mystery of God will be finished when the seventh angel begins to sound. The apostle Paul speaks of a mystery that was not revealed before Christ revealed it to him. He says that the mystery concerning the one body of Jew and Gentile saved apart from the law was "…in other ages was not made known unto the sons of men, as it is now revealed unto the apostles and prophets by the Spirit." (Eph. 3:5). However, the mystery revealed through Paul is not the mystery in view here in Revelation 10:7. This mystery has to do with prophecy (what the Old Testament prophets of Israel spoke about). So we ask "What is the mystery of God that is finished when the seventh angel begins to sound?" That mystery is simply that, before the kingdom can be set up, God has to judge and purge sin and unbelief from His people Israel. This is what John the Baptizer was talking about in Matthew 3:10-12.

John is commanded to eat the book
Revelation 10:8-11

"8 And the voice which I heard from heaven spake unto me again, and said, Go *and* take the little book which is open in the hand of the angel which standeth upon the sea and upon the earth. 9 And I went unto the angel, and said unto him, Give me the little book. And he said unto me, Take *it*, and eat it up; and it shall make thy belly bitter, but it shall be in thy mouth sweet as honey. 10 And I took the little book out of the angel's hand, and ate it up; and it was in my mouth sweet as honey: and as soon as I had eaten it, my belly was bitter. 11 And he said unto me, Thou must prophesy again before many peoples, and nations, and tongues, and kings." (Rev. 10:8-11)

In verse 8, John was told to eat the book which was sweet in his mouth but it made his belly bitter. His experience paralleled that of Ezekiel who was told to eat the roll in Ezekiel chapter 3 and tell its story to the house of Israel. The roll was sweet as honey in his mouth, but when he presented it to Israel, they would not listen. That is John's experience as well. The Word of God is sweet (Psalm 119:97-103) but when one presents it to people who are not interested, is makes the belly bitter.

Revelation Chapter 10 Study Guide Questions

1. Is the "another angel..." in verse 1, the sixth angel, the seventh angel, or is this a separate angel who is not one of the seven?

2. What should the reference to thunder in verse 3 remind us of? Consider Psalm 29 in your answer.

3. John was told not to write what the thunders uttered. Does this mean we will never know what the thunders said?

4. Verse 7 says "that there should be time no longer." Does this mean that time will cease to exist? What does it mean then? Does this have anything to do with the 42 months of Revelation 11:2?

5. What was it about the book in verse 10 that John was to eat that was sweet as honey in his mouth but made his belly bitter?

CHAPTER 11

The Lord's Two Witnesses Prophesy

John was to Measure the Temple

Revelation 11: 1-2

> "¹ And there was given me a reed like unto a rod: and the angel stood, saying, Rise, and measure the temple of God, and the altar, and them that worship therein. ² But the court which is without the temple leave out, and measure it not; for it is given unto the Gentiles: and the holy city shall they tread under foot forty *and* two months." (Rev. 11:1 & 2)

John is given a measuring stick and is told to measure the temple, the altar, and the people that worship in it. Taking a measure of something is what one does when he takes possession of it. Here, God is taking possession of the temple, the altar, and the people that worship in it. However, the outer court is not to be measured because it is to be given unto the Gentiles. This indicates that the time frame is after the rapture when God again deals with Israel as being separate from the Gentiles. Today, during the dispensation of grace, there is no distinction between the Jew and the Gentile (Eph. 2:13-18). In te tribulation period (the seventieth week of Daniel Chapter 9) Jerusalem is still regarded as the holy city even though it is trodden down of the Gentiles for 42 months yet. The 42 months is three and a half prophetic years (i.e. the second half of the seventieth week of Daniel 9). It is note worthy that the temple is rebuilt (Dan. 8 & 9) during the tribulation period and the temple service is re-established. However, the believing remnant of Israel will recognize that the temple service with its sacrifices no longer is the means of justification for them. Rather, the remnant will go to the book of Hebrews for their instruction on how to be right with God.

The Book of Hebrews presents the Lord Jesus Christ to Israel as her high priest who went into the temple of God in Heaven with His own blood as Israel's redeemer. Note that the Book of Hebrews presents the blood atonement of Christ in the context of Israel's program while the Book of Romans does that for us who live in the dispensation of grace. To go back to the blood sacrifices of the Old Testament would be to "crucify to themselves the Son of God afresh, and put *him* to an open shame" (Heb. 6:6).

Note the words in Hebrews: "Let us go forth therefore unto him without the camp…"

> Hebrews 13:10-13 ¹⁰ We have an altar, whereof they have no right to eat which serve the tabernacle. ¹¹ For the bodies of those beasts, whose blood is brought into the sanctuary by the high priest for sin, are burned without the camp. ¹² Wherefore Jesus also, that he might sanctify the people with his own blood, suffered without the gate. ¹³ Let us go forth therefore unto him without the camp, bearing his reproach.

Israel's Revive d Temple Service

It will be the making of the covenant between the antichrist and the unbelieving nation of Israel that begins the seventieth week (Dan. 9:27). It will then be the same antichrist that takes the daily sacrifice away (Dan. 8:9-11). In Daniel 8:13 we have information that enables us to calculate how long after the beginning of the seventieth week the temple is rebuilt. Daniel 8:13-14 "¹³ Then I heard one saint speaking, and another saint said unto that certain *saint* which spake, How long *shall be* the vision *concerning* the daily *sacrifice*, and the transgression of desolation, to give both the sanctuary and the host to be trodden under foot? ¹⁴ And he said unto me, Unto two thousand and three hundred days; then shall the sanctuary be cleansed." Take 7 years x 360 days per prophetic year = 2520 days. 2520 days – 2300 days =220 days. The temple will be reopened 220 days after the agreement of Daniel 9:27. The message of the believing remnant to the unbelieving nation will be: "Don't go to that temple because God is not there." The antichrist will cooperate in the rebuilding of the temple so that he can enter into it to proclaim himself to be God (Matt. 24:13 & 2Thess. 2:3&4). The believing remnant will know from passages as Psalm 141:1 & 2 what they must do when they do not have a temple service as in the case of those who were captive in Babylon.

> [1]LORD, I cry unto thee: make haste unto me; give ear unto my voice, when I cry unto thee. [2] Let my prayer be set forth before thee *as* incense; *and* the lifting up of my hands *as* the evening sacrifice. [3] Set a watch, O LORD, before my mouth; keep the door of my lips. [4] Incline not my heart to *any* evil thing, to practise wicked works with men that work iniquity: and let me not eat of their dainties. (Psalm 141:1-4)

God Empowers the Two Witnesses

Revelation 11:3-6

> "[3] And I will give *power* unto my two witnesses, and they shall prophesy a thousand two hundred *and* threescore days, clothed in sackcloth. [4] These are the two olive trees, and the two candlesticks standing before the God of the earth. [5] And if any man will hurt them, fire proceedeth out of their mouth, and devoureth their enemies: and if any man will hurt them, he must in this manner be killed. [6] These have power to shut heaven, that it rain not in the days of their prophecy: and have power over waters to turn them to blood, and to smite the earth with all plagues, as often as they will." (Rev. 11:3-6)

In this passage, the Lord has two witnesses who will prophecy 1260 days (3.5 years). Verse 4 makes reference to the two witnesses being the two olive trees and the two candlesticks standing before the God of the whole earth. This ties these two witnesses to Zechariah Chapter 4. The ministry of the two witnesses is to bring about the spiritual revival in Israel that will culminate in the calling out of the believing remnant. Who these two witnesses will be is speculation at this point. One is likely to be Elijah (Matt. 17:11). The other could be Moses (because the judgments brought about are similar to those brought on Egypt by Moses) or Enoch (who was translated so as not to see death before the judgment of the flood). There is however strong evidence that the two will be Moses and Elijah – the two that were with Jesus on the Mount of the Transfiguration.

The Lord tells the twelve that some among them would not see death until they see the Son of Man coming in his kingdom. That was in Matthew 16:28. Then in Matthew 17:3, the Lord is transfigured before them with Moses and Elijah on either side. Peter says that "…we … were eye witnesses of his majesty…" referring to the transfiguration (2Peter 1:16-18). In Malachi 4:4-6 the last two people listed in the Old Testament Scriptures are Moses and Elijah. The LORD tells Moses in Deuteronomy 18:18 "I will raise them up a Prophet from among their brethren, like unto thee, and will put my words in his mouth; and he shall speak unto them all that I shall command him" Israel was looking for Elijah and "That Prophet" (John 1:19-21). During the Lord's earthly ministry, Israel could have received the kingdom. If they would have received it, John the Baptist would have been Elijah (Matt. 17:9ff) and Jesus would have been the prophet like unto Moses. That is probably why the prophet like unto Moses is not named in Deuteronomy.

What about Enoch who did not die? Wouldn't he be a good candidate? Scripture says: "…It is appointed unto man once to die, but after this the judgment…" (Heb. 9:27). This however is speaking in general terms. There will be some in the rapture that never die (1Cor. 15:51). There are others such as Lazarus who died more than once.

It is interesting that the two witnesses stand before "the God of the earth." Before the captivity of Israel in Babylon, God was the God of all the earth (Psalm 47:7). However, after the captivity, He was the God of heaven (Ezra 1:2). Here He is again the God of all the earth because He is about to reclaim the earth.

The Beast Prevails Over the Two Witnesses

Revelation 11:7-8

> "⁷ And when they shall have finished their testimony, the beast that ascendeth out of the bottomless pit shall make war against them, and shall overcome them, and kill them. ⁸ And their dead bodies *shall lie* in the street of the great city, which spiritually is called Sodom and Egypt, where also our Lord was crucified." (Rev. 11:7-8)

Verse 7 speaks of a beast that ascends out of the bottomless pit. We discussed the bottomless pit in Revelation 9:1. The beast is the antichrist. In Revelation 9:11 we saw that there is a king over the bottomless pit. Revelation 17:8 describes him with the words: "⁸ The beast that thou sawest was, and is not; and shall ascend out of the bottomless pit, and go into perdition: and they that dwell on the earth shall wonder, whose names were not written in the book of life from the foundation of the world, when they behold the beast that was, and is not, and yet is." He was alive on earth at one time in that he "…was…" he was not alive at the time John wrote the Revelation in that he "…is not…" He will be alive again in that he "…yet is…" This person will be raised up again and when he is raised up, he will ascend out of the bottomless pit. In Revelation 13:1-3 we see an interesting parallel to this:

> "¹ And I stood upon the sand of the sea, and saw a beast rise up out of the sea,
>> having seven heads
>> and ten horns,
>> and upon his horns ten crowns,
>> and upon his heads the name of blasphemy.
> ² And the beast which I saw was like unto a leopard,
>>> and his feet were as *the feet* of a bear,
>>> and his mouth as the mouth of a lion:
> and the dragon gave him his power,
>> and his seat,
>> and great authority.
> ³ And I saw one of his heads as it were wounded to death;
>> and his deadly wound was healed:
>> and all the world wondered after the beast."

In 2Thessalonians 2:3 we see the antichrist referred to as "the man of sin" and "the son of perdition". In the first half of the seventieth week, he is referred to as the man of sin. In the second half, he becomes the son of perdition. Between the two, he dies. Zechariah 11:17 describes this apparent death and resurrection. He makes a deal with Satan in the bottomless pit. Satan then takes possession of his dead body much like Satan took possession of Judas. (John 13:27). It is only after he comes back as the son of perdition that he is able to kill the two witnesses. Judas was so totally possessed that he was referred to as the devil (John 6:70). Judas was not the devil but a man. His human father was named (John 6:71). So too the man of sin will be so totally possessed as to be genuinely the devil when he becomes the son of perdition. It is interesting that Judas was referred to as the son of perdition (John 17:12). The term "son of perdition" is a reference to a person that is totally under the control of the devil.

The World Rejoices over the Death of the Witnesses

Revelation 11:9-13

> "⁹ And they of the people and kindreds and tongues and nations shall see their dead bodies three days and an half, and shall not suffer their dead bodies to be put in graves. ¹⁰ And they that dwell upon the earth shall rejoice over them, and make merry, and shall send gifts one to another; because these two prophets tormented them that dwelt on the earth. ¹¹ And after three days and an half the Spirit of life from God entered into them, and they stood upon

their feet; and great fear fell upon them which saw them. [12] And they heard a great voice from heaven saying unto them, Come up hither. And they ascended up to heaven in a cloud; and their enemies beheld them. [13] And the same hour was there a great earthquake, and the tenth part of the city fell, and in the earthquake were slain of men seven thousand: and the remnant were affrighted, and gave glory to the God of heaven." (Rev. 11:9-13)

The people of the earth celebrate the death of these two witnesses. Here the beast becomes a hero to the people of the earth in that he destroyed them that had tormented them. The two witnesses are raised from the dead by God. They ascend to heaven in a cloud. A cloud is often a reference to a cloud of angels which is also accompanied with the voice of God (Exod. 14:19; Rev. 10:1; Acts 1:9; Matt. 24:30; 26:64; Mark 9:7; Mark. 13:26; 14:62; Luke 9:34; 21:27 Rev. 1:7; etc.). This marks the mid point of the Tribulation when the wrath of God is poured out on the inhabitants of the earth.

The Second Woe is Past

The Third Woe

Revelation 11:14-17

"[14] The second woe is past; *and*, behold, the third woe cometh quickly. [15] And the seventh angel sounded; and there were great voices in heaven, saying, The kingdoms of this world are become *the kingdoms* of our Lord, and of his Christ; and he shall reign for ever and ever. [16] And the four and twenty elders, which sat before God on their seats, fell upon their faces, and worshipped God, [17] Saying, We give thee thanks, O Lord God Almighty, which art, and wast, and art to come; because thou hast taken to thee thy great power, and hast reigned." (Rev. 11:14-17)

Here again are the twenty four elders (Rev. 4:4, 10; 5:8, 14). We see them whenever the focus is on God reclaiming the heaven and the earth back to Himself. Note also the contrast between Christ and the beast: Of Christ it is said "…which art, and wast, and art to come…" while of the beast it is said "he was, is not, and shall ascend…"

The Angry Nations and God's Wrath

Revelation 11:18

"[18] And the nations were angry, and thy wrath is come, and the time of the dead, that they should be judged, and that thou shouldest give reward unto thy servants the prophets, and to the saints, and them that fear thy name, small and great; and shouldest destroy them which destroy the earth." (Rev. 11:18)

Here the nations of the earth are angry at God (Psalm 2:1-3) and God is ready to pour out His wrath on them (Psalm 2:4). What a formula for conflict on a grand scale.

The Temple of God is opened in Heaven

Revelation 11:19

"[19] And the temple of God was opened in heaven, and there was seen in his temple the ark of his testament: and there were lightnings, and voices, and thunderings, and an earthquake, and great hail." (Rev. 11:19)

Cosmic disturbances in heaven coincide with God's wrath being ready to be poured out there. The temple of God can be then opened in heaven because of the events in Chapter 12:7ff. We see these cosmic disturbances prophesied in the Gospels and the Book of Acts.

"Then said he unto them, Nation shall rise against nation, and kingdom against kingdom. And great earthquakes shall be in diverse places, and famines, and pestilences; and fearful sights and great signs shall there be from heaven." (Luke 21:10-11)

"And I will show wonders in heaven above, and signs in the earth beneath, blood and fire, and vapor of smoke. The sun turned into darkness and moon into blood, before that great and notable day of the Lord come." (Acts 2:19-20)

Revelation Chapter 11 Study Guide Questions

1. What was John to measure and what was he not to measure in verses 1 and 2? What was this measuring activity a gesture of?

2. The mention of 42 months tells us where this is time wise. Where is this in the setting of the 70th week?

3. When will the temple be rebuilt relative to the 70th week? Will the believing remnant use the temple service? Why not?

4. Verses 3-6 tell of the impressive ministry of God's two witnesses. How long will their ministry be? Who do you think they might be? Why do you think so?

5. Verse 4 refers to God as the "God of the earth" while Ezra 1:2 refers to him as "the God of heaven". Before the captivity He was referred to as the God of the earth (Psalm 47:7). Why the change during the captivity? Why does the title change back to the God of the earth here in the Revelation?

6. What is the bottomless pit in Verse 7? Who is the beast that comes out of the pit?

7. The beast out of the bottomless pit succeeds in killing the two witnesses when no one else could. What is the reaction of the people of the world to this? What does this tell us of their spiritual state? What was God's response as we see it in Verses 12 and 13?

8. Verse 17 says of Christ "...which art and wast and art to come..." Compare this with what Revelation 13:1-3 says about the beast "he was, is not, and shall ascend." What does this say about each?

9. Why do you think the nations were angry as we see from Verse 18?

CHAPTER 12

A Woman Clothed with the Sun Lies in Travail
Revelation 12:1-2

> "¹ And there appeared a great wonder in heaven; a woman clothed with the sun, and the moon under her feet, and upon her head a crown of twelve stars: ² And she being with child cried, travailing in birth, and pained to be delivered." (Rev. 12:1-2)

These events actual happen on earth but the wonders appear in heaven before they happen on earth. The woman is (or represents, or is symbolic of) the nation of Israel.

- The significance of the reference to the sun and the moon and the twelve stars is seen by comparing this scene with Genesis 37:5-10. In verses 9 and 10 of that chapter we see Joseph's dream in which it was understood that the sun was Jacob, the moon was his wife, and the eleven stars were Joseph's sibling. The woman here clearly represents Israel.

- Israel is seen in Isaiah 54 as a woman married to the LORD.

- The Lord in John 16:19-22 likens Israel's time after He leaves as a woman in labor. He then speaks of a man being brought into the world in that day. Revelation 7:4 identifies the man child as the 144,000. The identification of the 144,000 as the man child reminds us of Ephesians 2:15 where we see the church - the body of Christ being so totally identified with Christ is to be called "the one new man." So too, in Revelation 7:4 the 144,000 is collectively identified as a man -- the man child of Revelation 12:5.

- The woman in the passage consists of all of the members of the nation of Israel that is in Palestine at the time of the Seventieth week. The Jews of the dispersion are not included. They will be gathered one by one later in the Book of the Revelation.

- There is an interesting passage on a man in travail as if in childbirth in Jeremiah 30:4-6 speaking about the time of Jacob's trouble (i.e. the tribulation). "⁴ And these *are* the words that the LORD spake concerning Israel and concerning Judah. ⁵ For thus saith the LORD; We have heard a voice of trembling, of fear, and not of peace. ⁶ Ask ye now, and see whether a man doth travail with child? wherefore do I see every man with his hands on his loins, as a woman in travail, and all faces are turned into paleness? ⁷ Alas! for that day *is* great, so that none *is* like it: it *is* even the time of Jacob's trouble; but he shall be saved out of it. ⁸ For it shall come to pass in that day, saith the LORD of hosts, *that* I will break his yoke from off thy neck, and will burst thy bonds, and strangers shall no more serve themselves of him: ⁹ But they shall serve the LORD their God, and David their king, whom I will raise up unto them." (Jer. 30:4-9)

- The purpose for the travail in pain is to produce new life. The believing remnant is the new life that is produced (cf. Heb. 12:18-22). Jeremiah 30:4-11 speaks of a man travailing as a woman with child during the time of Jacob's trouble (i.e. during the 70th week of Daniel Chapter 9). Paul speaks of the tribulation period as a time of tribulation as travail upon a woman with child in 1 Thessalonians 5:1).

- Isaiah 66:7-11 speaks of the birth of a man child before the travail came. Then, when she travailed, she brought forth her children. The man child is apparently the 144,000 of Revelation 7:4 but who are the children? The children then are the members of the believing remnant who are saved out of the nation. So we see in fore view the woman (Israel), the man child (the 144,000), and the children (the believing remnant of her seed). "⁷ Before she travailed, she brought forth; before her pain came, she was delivered of a man child. ⁸ Who hath heard such a thing? who hath seen such things? Shall the earth be made to bring forth in one day? or shall a nation be born at once? for as soon as Zion travailed, she brought forth her children. ⁹ Shall I bring to the birth, and not cause to bring forth? saith the LORD: shall I cause to bring forth, and shut *the womb*? saith thy God. ¹⁰ Rejoice ye with Jerusalem, and be glad with her, all ye that love her: rejoice for joy with her, all ye that mourn for her: [11] That ye may suck, and be satisfied with the breasts of her consolations; that ye may milk out, and be delighted with the abundance of her glory." (Isa. 66:7-11).

- The man child might also include the believers at Pentecost. They were also brought forth before the travail. Peter refers to them as "...a chosen generation, a royal priesthood, an holy nation..." (1Peter 2:9). This is the "nation" referred to in Matthew 21:43 – the nation that brings forth the fruit of Kingdom of God. It is also the "foolish nation" referred to in Romans 10:19 "[19] But I say, Did not Israel know? First Moses saith, I will provoke you to jealousy by *them that are* no people, *and* by a foolish nation I will anger you.".

- The man child is not Christ though many of the characteristics of the Lord Jesus Christ are applied to him. Christ had been born some 2,000 years plus before this. This man child will rule with Christ with a rod of iron when Christ reigns in His kingdom (verse 6). Note that Christ also will rule with a rod of iron (Rev. 19:11-15 cf. Psalm 110) but so will the over comers rule with Him (Rev. 2:27).

Satan, the Great Red Dragon, and the Man Child

Revelation 12:3-6

"[3] And there appeared another wonder in heaven; and behold a great red dragon, having seven heads and ten horns, and seven crowns upon his heads. [4] And his tail drew the third part of the stars of heaven, and did cast them to the earth: and the dragon stood before the woman which was ready to be delivered, for to devour her child as soon as it was born. [5] And she brought forth a man child, who was to rule all nations with a rod of iron: and her child was caught up unto God, and *to* his throne. [6] And the woman fled into the wilderness, where she hath a place prepared of God that they should feed her there a thousand two hundred *and* threescore days." (Rev. 12:3-6)

The dragon is representative of Satan and his man - the antichrist.

- The dragon is poised to destroy the man child.
- Comparing verse 3 with Revelation 13:1, it would appear that the dragon is intimately connected with the "Beast" - the antichrist.
- The dragon's tail draws one third of the stars of heaven and cast them to earth. This also personifies Satan and the stars represent the angels that followed him in rebellion against God. These angels being cast into the earth is seen in verse 9 where we see Satan and his angels cast into the earth. Though the fall in the angelic world happened after the original and before the fall of man, the casting of the fallen angles and the dragon does not happen until the middle of the tribulation period.
- An interesting study can be made of Leviathan with regard to Satan (Psalm 74:12-13; Isa. 26:16-27:1). Leviathan is presented as a very large sea dwelling creature in Job 41:1ff. However, studying the other passages on this creature, we begin to note some interesting things about him. He is somehow associated with Satan and the serpent. This reference to a serpent takes us back to Genesis 3 where it was the serpent that beguiled Eve (Gen. 3:13; 2Cor. 11:3). We would understand that it was not a snake that beguiled Eve but none other than Satan himself.
- Note that the antichrist (Rev. 13:1 & 2) comes out of the sea. The "sea" in Revelation 13 is likely a reference to the Middle East and the lands around the Mediterranean Sea. The antichrist will come from the Mediterranean area.

The man child (as we noted) is apparently the 144,000 of Revelation 7:4. This group will be caught up to God and His throne in the middle of the tribulation period by means of a mid-tribulation rapture / resurrection (verse 5). This is not to be confused with the rapture (or catching away) of the church the Body of Christ. These who are caught up Revelation 12:5 will return to earth with Christ 3.5 years later to reign (to rule with a rod of iron) with Him 1000 years. Those who were caught up in 1Thessalonians 4:17 are members of the church -- the body of Christ (the One New Man of Ephesians 2:15, those saved during the dispensation of grace) and will have changed and resurrection bodies that are "eternal in the heavens" (2Cor. 5:1) where they will ever (i.e. in the heavens) be at home with the Lord.

The woman of Revelation 12:6 is Israel. She flees into the wilderness where she is fed as Israel was fed in the wilderness during the exodus from Egypt. The antichrist's profaning of the temple is the sign that they were to look for the get out of Jerusalem (Matt. 24:13ff). The woman is fed 1260 days. That is 3.5 prophetic years of 360 days each (the second half of the tribulation period).

War in Heaven

Revelation 12:7-9

> "7 And there was war in heaven: Michael and his angels fought against the dragon; and the dragon fought and his angels, 8 And prevailed not; neither was their place found any more in heaven. 9 And the great dragon was cast out, that old serpent, called the Devil, and Satan, which deceiveth the whole world: he was cast out into the earth, and his angels were cast out with him." (Rev. 12:7-9)

Michael is the captain of armies of heaven. This is where the fallen angels are expelled from heaven. There are presently spiritual forces of wickedness out there (Eph. 6:12) in the heavens. These fallen angels are expelled so that the church which is Christ's body can take up positions of responsibility there. God is going to reconcile all things unto Himself both which are in heaven and which are in earth (Col. 1:20). He will do so by not only expelling the rebels who presently occupy the heavens but also to reconcile a body of believers to Himself to replace them (Col. 1:22). He has been doing this reconciling work for about 2,000 years so far. We members of the church which is His body will have a part in God restoring all things unto Himself (Eph. 1:4, 19-22; Col. 2:10). Our part (we who are members of the Church the Body of Christ) will be in the heavens (2Cor. 5:1-8) in celestial bodies (1Cor. 15:40) that will be fashioned after Christ's glorious body (Phil. 3:21) that can live there in the heavens and where we will reign with Christ for His honor and glory (2Tim. 2:12). The church which is Christ's Body will have been caught up to heaven at least 3.5 years earlier than this event. During this first three and a half years, the judgment seat of Christ will have been going on in heaven (Rom. 14:10 and 2Cor. 5:10) at which the fitness of individual members of the Body of Christ to reign in the heavens (2Tim. 2:10-15) will be determined by the judgment seat of Christ (2Cor. 5:9 & 10). When Satan and his angels are expelled from heaven by this event, the way is open for members of the Body of Christ to fill positions of responsibility in the heavens where they will reign with Christ (2Tim. 2:10-12).

Though all things in heaven and in earth are created by Christ and for Christ (Col. 1:16), both are in the hands of Satan today. Luke 4:6 and John 12:3 and 14:30 – 31 tell us that this earth is in his hands. Ephesians 2:2-3 tell us that the heavens are too. If we go back to Satan's original plot in Isaiah 14:12ff, we see that he had a five point plan:
1. He would ascend into heaven (i.e. It was an act of rebellion for him to ascend into heaven -- he was not created to be in heaven).
2. He will exalt his throne above the stars of heaven (i.e. he would rule over angels).
3. He would sit on the mount of the congregation (i.e. he would lead the government of the heavens).
4. He would ascend above the heights of the clouds (clouds refer to large companies of angels).
5. He would be like the most high (i.e. he would be like God). But verse 15 says "Yet thou shalt be brought down to hell to the sides of the pit."

This event (the casting out of Satan from heaven) happens in the middle of the Tribulation period. Here is when God purges the heavens of sin and rebellion. This takes us to Colossians 1:16-20 where we see that God will one day reconcile all things unto Himself whether they be things in heaven or things in earth. God will reconcile the things in heaven to Himself by removing the rebels there and replacing them with the body of Christ. Likewise, God will reconcile everything in this earth to Himself through redeemed Israel. But first, He has to expel the forces of wickedness. The event described in 2Corinthians 5:9&10 (the judgment seat of Christ) takes place during the first half of the Tribulation period. While the first half of the Tribulation rages on the earth, the judgment seat of Christ will be in session in the heavens. It is when the judgment seat of Christ closes that we members of the Body of Christ begin to reign in the heavens (2Tim 2:10-12) where we will judge angels (1Cor. 6:3).

The Third Woe to the Inhabiters of the Earth

Revelation 12:10-12

"10 And I heard a loud voice saying in heaven, Now is come salvation, and strength, and the kingdom of our God, and the power of his Christ: for the accuser of our brethren is cast down, which accused them before our God day and night. 11 And they overcame him by the blood of the Lamb, and by the word of their testimony; and they loved not their lives unto the death. 12 Therefore rejoice, *ye* heavens, and ye that dwell in them. Woe to the inhabiters of the earth and of the sea for the devil is come down unto you, having great wrath, because he knoweth that he hath but a short time." (Rev. 12:10-12)

These are the over comers of Revelation Chapters 1-3. They over came by the blood of the Lamb. The blood atonement for Israel is presented to them in the Book of Hebrews (Heb. 9:12). In Hebrews 12:18 – 29 the Hebrew people are instructed to go on the New Covenant and not go back to the old. It will be the antichrist that will set up and reinstitute the Old Testament blood sacrifices. Hebrews tells them to not go back to these Old Testament sacrifices. Hebrews 6:1-4 can be understood if we understand that "those who were once enlightened, and have tasted of the heavenly gift, and were made partakers of the Holy Ghost…" were Israelites at Pentecost in Acts Chapters 2 through 5 who could turn back to the Old Covenant instead of going on to the New Covenant.

At this point, they that dwell in the heavens will include the elect angels and us the members of the church the body of Christ. The inhabiters of the earth are in for the fierce wrath of Satan because he knows that he now has only 1260 days left to the showdown with Christ. It is here that Satan apparently first begins to realize that he could loose in his conflict with Christ in that he loses his position in the heavens. His wrath intensifies against the inhabitants of the earth from here to the end. Note that the "woe" of Revelation 12:12 is the third woe of Revelation 8:13.

The Red Dragon Pursues the Women

Revelation 12:13-17

"13 And when the dragon saw that he was cast unto the earth, he persecuted the woman which brought forth the man *child*. 14 And to the woman were given two wings of a great eagle, that she might fly into the wilderness, into her place, where she is nourished for a time, and times, and half a time [three and a half years], from the face of the serpent. 15 And the serpent cast out of his mouth water as a flood after the woman, that he might cause her to be carried away of the flood. 16 And the earth helped the woman, and the earth opened her mouth, and swallowed up the flood which the dragon cast out of his mouth. 17 And the dragon was wroth with the woman, and went to make war with the remnant of her seed, which keep the commandments of God, and have the testimony of Jesus Christ." (Rev. 12:13-17)

The woman (Israel) will be given a place to hide in the wilderness that will be beyond the reach of the antichrist. The lands of ancient Edom, Moab, and parts of Ammon will escape dominion of the antichrist (Dan. 11:41). Israel will be nourished there as she was in the 40 years of wondering in the Exodus. After that the woman is beyond reach, the antichrist will direct his efforts on destroying the believing remnant of her seed. Here is where Matthew 25:31-46 comes into the picture. The Gentiles who enter the Kingdom do so because they protected, hid and fed the remnant scattered throughout the world.

Matthew 25:31-46 (KJV)

[31] When the Son of man shall come in his glory, and all the holy angels with him, then shall he sit upon the throne of his glory: [32] And before him shall be gathered all nations: and he shall separate them one from another, as a shepherd divideth *his* sheep from the goats: [33] And he shall set the sheep on his right hand, but the goats on the left. [34] Then shall the King say unto them on his right hand, Come, ye blessed of my Father, inherit the kingdom prepared for you from the foundation of the world: [35] For I was an hungred, and ye gave me meat: I was thirsty, and ye gave me drink: I was a stranger, and ye took me in: [36] Naked, and ye clothed me: I was sick, and ye visited me: I was in prison, and ye came unto me.

[37] Then shall the righteous answer him, saying, Lord, when saw we thee an hungred, and fed *thee*? or thirsty, and gave *thee* drink? [38] When saw we thee a stranger, and took *thee* in? or naked, and clothed *thee*? [39] Or when saw we thee sick, or in prison, and came unto thee? [40] And the King shall answer and say unto them, Verily I say unto you, Inasmuch as ye have done *it* unto one of the least of these my brethren, ye have done *it* unto me. [41] Then shall he say also unto them on the left hand, Depart from me, ye cursed, into everlasting fire, prepared for the devil and his angels: [42] For I was an hungred, and ye gave me no meat: I was thirsty, and ye gave me no drink: [43] I was a stranger, and ye took me not in: naked, and ye clothed me not: sick, and in prison, and ye visited me not.

[44] Then shall they also answer him, saying, Lord, when saw we thee an hungred, or athirst, or a stranger, or naked, or sick, or in prison, and did not minister unto thee? [45] Then shall he answer them, saying, Verily I say unto you, Inasmuch as ye did *it* not to one of the least of these, ye did *it* not to me. [46] And these shall go away into everlasting punishment: but the righteous into life eternal.

Revelation Chapter 12 Study Guide Questions

1. Who does the woman in verse 1 represent? Why do you think so?

2. Who does the child that the woman in verse 2 is expecting represent?

3. Who does the great red dragon in verse 3 represent?

4. Who do the stars in verse 4 that the dragon's tail drew from heaven represent?

5. Who does the man child in verse 5 represent?

6. Why did the dragon want to devour the man child?

7. What is the wilderness that the woman flees to?

8. What verse in Ephesians indicates that Satan is in heaven yet today?

9. How does the time frame of the war in heaven in verse 7 relate to the event we call the rapture?

10. How does the war in heaven relate to the time frame of the tribulation period?

11. Why is there a woe to the inhabitants of the earth in verse 12?

12. Who is the woman and who is the remnant of her seed in verse 17?

CHAPTER 13

A beast arises out of the sea, and the dragon gives it his power
Revelation 13:1-2

> "1 And I stood upon the sand of the sea, and saw a beast rise up out of the sea, having seven heads and ten horns, and upon his horns ten crowns, and upon his heads the name of blasphemy. 2 And the beast which I saw was like unto a leopard, and his feet were as *the feet* of a bear, and his mouth as the mouth of a lion: and the dragon gave him his power, and his seat, and great authority." (Rev. 13:1-2)

In Revelation 12:3 we encountered a great red dragon having seven heads and ten horns. Now in Revelation 13:1, we meet a beast arising out of the sea having seven heads and ten horns and upon his heads the name of blasphemy. Here in chapter 13 we will meet the unholy trinity.

1. The great red dragon – the devil, the unholy father
2. The beast out of the sea – the false messiah (a man) the antichrist (a political leader)
3. The beast out of the land – the false spirit (a religious leader) the false prophet.

The seven heads appear in Revelation 12:3; 13:1; 17:3, 7, 12, 16. The seven heads are explained in Revelation 17:10. The seven heads are "...seven kings: five are fallen, one is, and the other is not yet come..." These are seven kings (or kingdoms) that have in the past or will in the future oppress Israel.

Five are fallen:

    1. Egypt
    2. Syria
    3. Babylon
    4. Media Persia
    5. Greece

One is:

    6. Rome

Another is yet to come:

    7. The man of sin

Then there is an eighth that is of the seven:

    8. "And the beast that was and is not, even he is the eighth, and is of the seven, and goeth into perdition." More on this guy later.

The ten horns appear in Daniel 7:7, 20, 24; Revelation 12:3; 13:1; 17:3, 7, 12, 16. The ten horns are ten kings that reign with the antichrist. They correspond with the ten toes of Daniel 2:41.

The beast is part like a leopard, part like a bear, and part like a lion. This takes us back to Daniel chapter 7. There Daniel saw in a night vision (night referring to the times of the Gentiles – it can also refer to the time when the Lord is not present with Israel as in John 9:4) a series of beasts come up in succession. Note from Daniel 7:2 that the four winds of the heaven strove upon the great sea. The term "winds" suggest that there are spirit forces involved. The term "the great sea" suggests that this is happening around the Mediterranean Sea. These are kingdoms that arise in the Mediterranean area. It is interesting to note also that the term "waters" according to Revelation 17:15 also refers to people, multitudes, nations, and tongues. Thus it is referring to the Gentile world system. We can identify the four beasts from information in Daniel Chapter 7 as noted below:

1. The first beast in Daniel 7 is like a lion. Studying Jeremiah 4:7 and comparing with 25:9 we see that the lion is Babylon. So too the reference to eagles wings when studied in light of Ezekiel 17:3 & 12 also associates the first beast of Daniel 7 with Babylon.

2. The second was like a bear. This is apparently the Persian Empire. The three ribs would be Babylon, Media, and Persia -- three kingdoms that become sxwallowed up by Persia.

3. The third beast was like a leopard. This apparently represents Greece. The wings speak of the speed of conquest of Alexander the Great. The four wings and the four heads speak of the four generals who divided the kingdom among themselves (Daniel 8:22) after Alexander's death. The Greek empire divided into Macedonia, Thrace, Syria, and Egypt (Ptolemy). In Daniel 8:8-9, we see that the antichrist comes out of one of the fourfold division of the Greek empire.

4. The fourth beast becomes the focus of Daniel's interest. It was dreadful and terrible and strong exceedingly. It had great iron teeth. It was diverse from all the others beasts that were before. It shall devour the whole earth, and shall tread it down, and break it in pieces (Dan. 7:23). Also, it had ten horns. A horn is a kingdom (Rev. 17:8-12). In Daniel 11 we see that the antichrist is the king of the north (Syria). This king will have his way until Christ comes. He will not care for the God of his fathers (i.e. he will be of Jewish descent). He will magnify himself above all. He will magnify the god of forces. He will honor a god his fathers knew not (he will honor Satan). He shall cause them (i.e. the ten kings) to rule over many and shall divide the land for gain. (Dan. 11:38ff)

Note from Daniel 7:17 that these are four kings that <u>shall be</u>. The first kingdom already was when Daniel gets this vision. (Dan. 7:1). Note also that the ten horns are also ten kings that shall arise (Dan 7:24). Note also that all four will be on earth at the same time (Dan. 7:12). It appears that Babylon (Iraq), Media-Persia (Iran), Greece, and Rome (or perhaps Assyria) will again be players in the end time events. It is clear that the fourth beast is the kingdom of the antichrist. This beast starts out as a ten nation confederacy (Psalm 83:1-8). Another horn (kingdom) comes up among them. He comes up among the ten and conquers three of them (Dan. 7:8).

Satan finally gets the worship that he had been seeking

Revelation 13:3-4
"³ And I saw one of his heads as it were wounded to death; and his deadly wound was healed: and all the world wondered after the beast. ⁴ And they worshipped the dragon which gave power unto the beast: and they worshipped the beast, saying, Who *is* like unto the beast? who is able to make war with him?" (Rev. 13:3-4)

The fourth beast had one of its heads wounded to death but that deadly wound was healed. In Zechariah 11:15-17 the prophet talks about the wounds of the idol shepherd. This is prophetic of the wounding of the beast that we see here in Revelation 13. See also Psalm 10:15.

Satan is the great imitator of God. It is an interesting study to compare the work of Christ and that of Satan and the antichrist. The table in the close of Chapter 6 lays out that comparison.

The three and a half year career of the antichrist – the man of sin

Revelation 13:5-6
"⁵ And there was given unto him a mouth speaking great things and blasphemies; and power was given unto him to continue forty *and* two months. ⁶ And he opened his mouth in

blasphemy against God, to blaspheme his name, and his tabernacle, and them that dwell in heaven." (Rev. 13:5-6)

Here again we find the 42 months or 3.5 years. This is the second half of the Tribulation Period. Among the people in heaven at the time that this takes place will be us members of the church the Body of Christ.

The Antichrist Gains World wide Worship

Revelation 13:7-10

"[7] And it was given unto him to make war with the saints, and to overcome them: and power was given him over all kindreds, and tongues, and nations. [8] And all that dwell upon the earth shall worship him, whose names are not written in the book of life of the Lamb slain from the foundation of the world. [9] If any man have an ear, let him hear. [10] He that leadeth into captivity shall go into captivity: he that killeth with the sword must be killed with the sword. Here is the patience and the faith of the saints." (Rev. 13:7-10)

There will be people in every nation who worship the antichrist. These will be people whose names are not in the Book of Life. See the notes at the end of Chapter three on the Book of Life. The patience of the saints in verse 10 is the assurance that God is going to bring recompense on those who lead Israel into captivity and those who kill by the sword. Those who take the believers captive will be taken captive and those who kill by the sword will die by the sword.

A second beast causes an image to be made of the first

Revelation 13:11-17

"[11] And I beheld another beast coming up out of the earth; and he had two horns like a lamb, and he spake as a dragon. [12] And he exerciseth all the power of the first beast before him, and causeth the earth and them which dwell therein to worship the first beast, whose deadly wound was healed. [13] And he doeth great wonders, so that he maketh fire come down from heaven on the earth in the sight of men, [14] And deceiveth them that dwell on the earth by *the means of* those miracles which he had power to do in the sight of the beast; saying to them that dwell on the earth, that they should make an image to the beast, which had the wound by a sword, and did live. [15] And he had power to give life unto the image of the beast, that the image of the beast should both speak, and cause that as many as would not worship the image of the beast should be killed. [16] And he causeth all, both small and great, rich and poor, free and bond, to receive a mark in their right hand, or in their foreheads: [17] And that no man might buy or sell, save he that had the mark, or the name of the beast, or the number of his name." (Rev. 13: 11-17)

The second beast is a religious leader who is also associated with the great red dragon. This is the false prophet of Revelation 16:13. He uses a religious system to keep people in darkness. He uses miracles to deceive people in the entire world to worship the beast. He uses the occasion of the death and apparent resurrection of the first beast as a means to control people by means of religious deception through a religious system that he creates. The religious system is probably going to be like the one that was developed by Micah in Judges 17:1ff. In Judges 18, we see that the tribe of Dan put that system over the entire tribe (cf. Gen. 49:16 & 17).

The second beast makes an image to the first beast. This is an imitation of the work of the Holy Spirit who directs worship to Christ (John 14:26). He also imitates the work of Elijah (Note the Respect for Abel's offering. Also see 1Chronicles 21:25 and Leviticus 9:23 and 10:1 on how God accepts offerings by fire). The second beast calls fire down from heaven in imitation of God in 2Chronicles 7:1. One of the greatest dangers to one's faith is to believe what one sees in disregard to what the Word of God says. In Deuteronomy 13:1-4 the LORD warns Israel not to believe what is seen if what is seen is different from what the Word of God says. The Word of God is the final authority.

- Mathew 7:22 speaks of many who will have prophesied in His name and cast out devils in His name and done wonderful works in His name but were lost people who were workers on iniquity.
- In Acts 19:13 we see vagabond Jews who were exorcists.
- Second Timothy 3:8 speaks of Jannes and Jambres who worked miracles by black magic.

Paul tells us what the source is of the false prophet's power to do miracles. It is the working of Satan. "⁹ *Even him*, whose coming is after the working of Satan with all power and signs and lying wonders, ¹⁰ And with all deceivableness of unrighteousness in them that perish; because they received not the love of the truth, that they might be saved. ¹¹ And for this cause God shall send them strong delusion, that they should believe a lie: ¹² That they all might be damned who believed not the truth, but had pleasure in unrighteousness." (2Thess. 2:9-12)

This is the source of the signs and wonders ministries today. Paul tells us that when the Word of God is complete (when complete knowledge and complete prophecy comes), then the gift of prophecy will fail, the gift of tongues will cease, and the gift of supernatural knowledge will vanish away (1Cor. 13:8) to be replaced by the completed Word of God. Tongues served a purpose as a sign to Israel that their promised Kingdom is being offered to them (1Cor. 1:22; 14:22; John 4:48). God used tongues as a sign to the unbelieving nation in Acts Chapters 2 through 4 as a sign that the one the nation crucified was their Messiah. The message preached by Peter and the twelve to Israel was that Jesus is the Christ and that the kingdom was being offered to them. The Holy Spirit was offering the Kingdom to Israel during the first seven chapter s of the Book of Acts. If the nation would have repented of their deed of crucifying their Messiah, then God would have sent Jesus back and the kingdom would have been establish. They however stood by their deed and rejected this offer by stoning Stephen.

God used tongues as a sign to Israel again when the tongues among the Gentiles at Corinth was a sign to Israel that God was now working with the Gentiles and not with Israel. The message that Israel should have gotten from what was happening at Corinth was that God was now working among the Gentiles and not in Israel. A dispensational change had taken place.

The mark of the beast: The "all" of verse 16 is all in the antichrist's kingdom. This does not necessarily mean that everyone on earth will have to take the mark of the beast in order to carry on business. In the Middle East; Edom, Moab and Ammon will escape the conquest of the antichrist (Dan. 11:40-42). This action by the beast will follow the social credit system being implemented in China and other totalitarian states in the world today.

Though the antichrist influences the entire world, his kingdom extends only to the ten nations represented by the ten toes of the great image in Daniel Chapter 2.Those that take the mark of the beast will not escape the wrath of God (Prov. 13:13). This wrath will be revealed at the separation of the sheep from the goats (Matt. 25:32). Those that survive the attack on Jerusalem will go up to the feast of Tabernacles every year (Zech. 14:16-21).

The Number of the Beast

Revelation 13:18

"[18] Here is wisdom. Let him that hath understanding count the number of the beast: for it is the number of a man; and his number *is* Six hundred threescore *and* six."(Rev. 13:18)

The beast has a number associated with his name. In the Greek as in the Latin, numbers are represented by letters. Therefore, it is probable that the Tribulation saints will be able to identify the beast by adding the numbers of his name. As an illustration (and note that this is only meant to be an illustration) of this, consider the Latin title for the Pope:

$$
\begin{array}{ll}
V & = 5 \\
I & = 1 \\
C & = 100 \\
I & = 1 \\
V & = 5 \\
I & = 1 \\
L & = 50 \\
I & = 1 \\
I & = 1 \\
D & = 500 \\
I & = 1 \\
\hline
\text{Total} & = 666
\end{array}
$$

An interesting study can be made of the number 666 in Scripture. It occurs often – always in association with the working of Satan. The form of the number 666 as a triplet is in itself interesting. Six is the number for man (man was created on the sixth day of creation week) while three is the number for the trinity--- for God. The antichrist is a man who claims to be God and uses an unholy trinity to do so.

Revelation 13 Study Guide Questions

1. How does the beast that rose up out of the sea in verse 1 relate to the red dragon we saw in Revelation 12:3 (aside from the fact that both have seven heads and ten horns).

2. List the members of the unholy Trinity.

3. Who (what countries/nations) do the seven heads represent?

4. What is the significance of one of the heads of the beast bring wounded to death?

5. What impressed people about the beast in verse 4 of this chapter that compelled worship?

6. What is significant about the 42 months of verse 5?

CHAPTER 14

The Lamb stands on Mount Sion with the company of His elect
Revelation 14:12

> ""¹ And I looked, and, lo, a Lamb stood on the mount Sion, and with him an hundred forty *and* four thousand, having his Father's name written in their foreheads. ² And I heard a voice from heaven, as the voice of many waters, and as the voice of a great thunder: and I heard the voice of harpers harping with their harps:" (Rev.14:1-2)

This scene takes place in heaven. In verse 4 we see that these 144,000 are the first fruits of the coming harvest of the redeemed of Israel (See 1Cor. 15:23 and; James 1:18 on the term first fruits). These 144,000 are a counterpart to the twelve apostles. These 144,000 comprise what was called the manchild in Revelation 12:5 which was caught up to God in the middle of the tribulation period. This begins the actual establishment of the Kingdom of Heaven. There was an offer of the Kingdom made to Israel by the Holy Spirit through Peter and the twelve apostles in the first seven chapters Book of Acts. There is a correspondence between what was offered then and what is happening here in the Revelation. Note the correspondence:

First Advent	Second Advent
Twelve Apostles	144,000
Little Flock (Believers at Pentecost)	The Believing Remnant
Two men prophesied to come: Prophet like unto Moses (that prophet being Christ)	The two witnesses Moses
John (Came in the spirit of Elijah)	Elijah

God inaugurated the New Covenant through the twelve. The bringing in of the New Covenant was interrupted by the Dispensation of Grace. After the rapture (the catching away of the Body of Christ to Heaven), it will be re-inaugurated through the 144,000. The Book of Hebrews teaches the spiritual effect of the New Covenant as it will be applied to Israel during the tribulation period.

There are three metaphors of Abraham's innumerable seed that we find in the Bible:
- Seed as numerous as the stars of heaven (Gen. 15:5; 22:17; 26:4) -- probably representative of the Body of Christ in heaven.
- Seed as numerous as the sand of the sea shore (Gen. 22:17; Josh. 11:4; 1Sam. 13:5 Heb. 11:12) – perhaps representative of the nation of Israel (the Israel of God being God's earthly people).
- As numerous as the dust of the earth (Gen. 13:16; 28:14) -- perhaps representing the Gentiles saved during the coming Kingdom of Heaven.

The 144,000 sing a New Song

Revelation 14:3

> "³ And they sung as it were a new song before the throne, and before the four beasts, and the elders: and no man could learn that song but the hundred *and* forty *and* four thousand, which were redeemed from the earth." (Rev. 14:3)

The 144,000 sang a new song. There are a number of times in the Bible that people sang a new song. Most of the songs are in the Psalms. Moses sang a new song after Israel crossed the Red Sea in Exodus 15:1. He sang another before Israel crossed the Jordan into the Promised Land (Duet. 31:22). The twenty four elders sang a new song in Chapter 5. All of the new songs in the Bible are in some way connected with redemption. This song in verse 3 only the 144,000 could learn. This is apparently a song whereby one has to have suffered through the experience of the theme of it in order to sing it. Even the Lord Himself had to suffer to learn some things and come to maturity as Israel's High Priest (Heb. 5:6-9).

The 144,000 are the first fruits to God

Revelation 14:4-5

> "4 These are they which were not defiled with women; for they are virgins. These are they which follow the Lamb whithersoever he goeth. These were redeemed from among men, *being* the firstfruits unto God and to the Lamb. 5 And in their mouth was found no guile: for they are without fault before the throne of God." (Rev. 14:4-5)

The reference to not being defiled with women is not a reference being celibate. Hebrews 13:4 says "Marriage is honorable in all and the bed undefiled..." There is nothing immoral or defiling about sex in marriage. The Bible uses fornication as a metaphor for idolatry. We see this in Revelation 2:14 where we find that Balaam taught Israel to eat things sacrificed to idols and to thereby commit fornication. Fornication in that sense has to do with being associated with religious systems that use idolatry to keep people from the truth and from repentance and from worship of the one true God.

In Numbers 25:1-5 we find Israel committing fornication with the daughters of Moab by eating things sacrificed unto their gods and to join themselves unto Baal worship. The doctrine of Balaam is connected with the religious system of the antichrist. These virgins in Revelation 14 are Israelites who will have nothing to do with the religious system of the antichrist.

In Revelation 2:20 we saw a reference to a Jezebel who will be there during the Tribulation Period and will call herself a prophetess and will teach Israel to commit fornication with idols. The historic Jezebel was a daughter of a priest of Baal. This Jezebel will apparently be a Baal worshiper also. It is likely that the religion of the antichrist will be Baal worship.

In light of this, the parable in Matthew 25:1-13 is interesting. Ten is the number representative of the Gentiles. They in Matthew 25 are Jews who are ministering to the Gentiles during the Tribulation. The fact that they are virgins is a testimony that they are free of the religion of the antichrist. Five of them were ready but the other five were not. It was said of them who were not ready that they lacked sufficient oil. Oil is a type of the Holy Spirit. Hebrews 6:4 talks about Hebrews who went part way with the Holy Ghost but not all the way. It will take total commitment to the gospel of the kingdom and the New Covenant for an Israelite to get through the tribulation and into the kingdom.

An angel preaches the gospel

Revelation 14:6-7

> "6 And I saw another angel fly in the midst of heaven, having the everlasting gospel to preach unto them that dwell on the earth, and to every nation, and kindred, and tongue, and people, 7 Saying with a loud voice, Fear God, and give glory to him; for the hour of his judgment is come: and worship him that made heaven, and earth, and the sea, and the fountains of waters." (Rev.14:6-7)

Here we find an angel preaching a gospel. It is called the everlasting gospel. The message of this gospel is that if you fear God and give him the glory, you will escape the coming judgment (verse 7). This is different than the gospel of the grace of God that Paul preached. Interestingly, Paul says "But though we, or an angel from heaven, preach any other gospel unto you than that which we have preached unto you, let him be accursed." (Gal. 1:8) But here we see an angel from heaven preaching another gospel than the gospel of the grace of God that Paul preached and was not cursed. In fact Peter preached a different gospel than Paul preached (Gal. 2:6-9) and was called of Christ to do so. The key to understanding this is that neither the angel nor Peter was working in the same program as Paul. The angel is in the prophetic program while Paul is in the mystery program (Rom. 16:25; Eph. 3:2; 1Cor. 2:8; etc.).

The gospel that Paul preached is that "Christ died for our sins..." (1Cor. 15:1-4). The gospel that Peter preached is that if Israel would repent of the deed of crucifying their Messiah and be baptized for the remission of their sins, Christ would return and they would have their sins "...blotted out when the times of refreshing shall come from the presence of the Lord; And he shall send Jesus Christ, which before was preached unto you: Whom the heaven must receive until the times of restitution of all things, which God hath spoken by the mouth of all his holy prophets since the world began." (Acts 3:19-21) For us living in the Dispensation of Grace, we are now justified, reconciled, and have received the atonement the moment we trust the death burial and resurrection of Christ for our redemption. (Rom. 5:8). Israel will, as a covenant nation, receive their atonement at the close of the tribulation when the Lord Jesus comes to that nation as her Messiah.

The Fall of Babylon

Revelation 14:8
> "⁸ And there followed another angel, saying, Babylon is fallen, is fallen, that great city, because she made all nations drink of the wine of the wrath of her fornication." (Rev. 14:8)

Here we see the final fall of Babylon. This fall was prophesied in Jeremiah 50 and 51. Babylon will never be rebuilt or inhabited again after it is destroyed (Jer. 50:39-41; 51:7-9). When Peter wrote First Peter, there was a church in Babylon (1Pet 5:8) and in fact Peter was ministering to that church. We understand then that the prophesied destruction has not happened yet. Revelation 14 establishes the time frame of the prophesied destruction. There is currently a small population at the site of ancient Babylon. However, it will have to be rebuilt and become a center of commerce for this prophecy to be fulfilled. Revelation 17 and 18 describes a future earthly glory of this city and its final actual, ultimate destruction.

The Dire Warning of the Third Angel

Revelation 14:9-12
> "⁹ And the third angel followed them, saying with a loud voice, If any man worship the beast and his image, and receive *his* mark in his forehead, or in his hand, ¹⁰ The same shall drink of the wine of the wrath of God, which is poured out without mixture into the cup of his indignation; and he shall be tormented with fire and brimstone in the presence of the holy angels, and in the presence of the Lamb: ¹¹ And the smoke of their torment ascendeth up for ever and ever: and they have no rest day nor night, who worship the beast and his image, and whosoever receiveth the mark of his name. ¹² Here is the patience of the saints: here *are* they that keep the commandments of God, and the faith of Jesus." (Rev. 14:9-12)

To worship the beast and his image and take his mark will bring the wrath of God on these people in the Tribulation. Such will be tormented with fire and brimstone in the presence of the holy angels and the Lamb. Compare this with 2Thessalonians 1:9 where the punishment is "...from the presence of the Lord..." This is the Gehenna fire that can destroy both body and soul (Mark 9:43-49; Matt. 5:29 & 30). Mark 9:49 speaks of being salted with fire. Salt is a preservative while fire inflicts suffering and destruction. This is fire that preserves so that people in it do not cease to suffer the wrath of God. In Revelation 19:20, the beast is cast alive into that fire. In Revelation 20:10, Satan is cast into it and the beast is still there, he was not annihilated though he was placed there 1,000 years earlier. This is truly the wrath of God poured without mixture and without dilution. How blessed it is to experience the love and mercy and grace of God. It is Christ who endured the wrath of God against the sin of the believer. If you the reader have never trusted in the redeeming work of Jesus Christ, do so now.

The Blessing of the Martyred Dead

Revelation 14:13

"¹³ And I heard a voice from heaven saying unto me, Write, Blessed *are* the dead which die in the Lord from henceforth: Yea, saith the Spirit, that they may rest from their labours; and their works do follow them." (Rev. 14:13)

Those that die in the Lord at any time are blessed. These are particularly blessed because they escape the horrors of the Great Tribulation.

Revelation 14:14-16

"¹⁴ And I looked, and behold a white cloud, and upon the cloud *one* sat like unto the Son of man, having on his head a golden crown, and in his hand a sharp sickle. ¹⁵ And another angel came out of the temple, crying with a loud voice to him that sat on the cloud, Thrust in thy sickle, and reap: for the time is come for thee to reap; for the harvest of the earth is ripe. ¹⁶ And he that sat on the cloud thrust in his sickle on the earth; and the earth was reaped." (Rev. 14:14-16)

Verses 13 through 20 speak of the harvest of the earth. There are two harvests. One is the harvest of the people of the earth (verses 14-16). This is the separation of the sheep from the goats (Matt. 25:32) among the Gentiles and the separation or the wheat from the chaff among the Israelites (Matt. 3:12). The parable of the sower in Matthew 13:33-43 speaks of this event also. The other harvest is the harvest of the cluster of the vine of the earth (Verses 17 thru 20). Deuteronomy 32:31-37 gives us a clue to enable us to understand what this vine of the earth is. Just as there is a true Rock (that being Christ) and a false rock, so there is a true vine (John 15:4 & 5) and a false vine. The false vine is the system of idolatry that started back in Babel. What started at Babel in Genesis Chapter 11 was man creating a culture with an economic, political and religious system that was specifically design to exclude God from planet earth. That vine finally manifests itself in the worship of the antichrist. The first harvest (of the people) results in a separation of the believers from the unbelievers. The fruit of the second harvest (of the unbelievers) is totally crushed in the "...great winepress of the wrath of God (verse 19). Isaiah 63:1-6 is a prophecy of this event. Jeremiah 25:31-33 speaks of this as well "³¹ A noise shall come *even* to the ends of the earth; for the LORD hath a controversy with the nations, he will plead with all flesh; he will give them *that are* wicked to the sword, saith the LORD. ³² Thus saith the LORD of hosts, Behold, evil shall go forth from nation to nation, and a great whirlwind shall be raised up from the coasts of the earth. ³³ And the slain of the LORD shall be at that day from *one* end of the earth even unto the *other* end of the earth: they shall not be lamented, neither gathered, nor buried; they shall be dung upon the ground."

The Winepress of the Wrath of God

Revelation 14:17-20

"¹⁷ And another angel came out of the temple which is in heaven, he also having a sharp sickle. ¹⁸ And another angel came out from the altar, which had power over fire; and cried with a loud cry to him that had the sharp sickle, saying, Thrust in thy sharp sickle, and gather the clusters of the vine of the earth; for her grapes are fully ripe. ¹⁹ And the angel thrust in his sickle into the earth, and gathered the vine of the earth, and cast *it* into the great winepress of the wrath of God. ²⁰ And the winepress was trodden without the city, and blood came out of the winepress, even unto the horse bridles, by the space of a thousand *and* six hundred furlongs." (Rev. 14:17-20)

As we noted in the paragraph above, this is the gathering of the vine of the earth (the false system of worship) that is totally crushed in the winepress of the wrath of God.

The "…blood came out of the winepress, even unto the horses bridles…" by the space of 1600 furlongs (verse 20). The distance of 1600 furlongs is a distance of over 184 miles. Zechariah 1:8-17 will help us understand how that could be. We see in the Zechariah passage that the blood is splashed up from the hooves of horses that carry the Lord and His angels when He comes to avenge Israel. This is talking about an event in the tribulation period when the Lord finally vents His wrath.

Zechariah 1:8-17 (KJV) This passage is prophetic of the Lord at His return to earth at the close of the Tribulation.

> "[8] I saw by night, and behold a man riding upon a red horse, and he stood among the myrtle trees that *were* in the bottom; and behind him *were there* red horses, speckled, and white. [The rider on the first red horse is Christ. The next horses are ridden by the angels that accompany Him. Their horses are speckled. Further down the line are the white horses.]

> [9] Then said I, O my lord, what *are* these? And the angel that talked with me said unto me, I will shew thee what these *be*. [10] And the man that stood among the myrtle trees answered and said, These *are they* whom the LORD hath sent to walk to and fro through the earth. [11] And they answered the angel of the LORD that stood among the myrtle trees, and said, We have walked to and fro through the earth, and, behold, all the earth sitteth still, and is at rest.

> [12] Then the angel of the LORD answered and said, O LORD of hosts, how long wilt thou not have mercy on Jerusalem and on the cities of Judah, against which thou hast had indignation these threescore and ten years? [Three score and ten would be the 70 year long period of the captivity.][13] And the LORD answered the angel that talked with me *with* good words *and* comfortable words. [14] So the angel that communed with me said unto me, Cry thou, saying, Thus saith the LORD of hosts; I am jealous for Jerusalem and for Zion with a great jealousy. [15] And I am very sore displeased with the heathen *that are* at ease: for I was but a little displeased, and they helped forward the affliction.

> [16] Therefore thus saith the LORD; I am returned to Jerusalem with mercies: my house shall be built in it, saith the LORD of hosts, and a line shall be stretched forth upon Jerusalem. [17] Cry yet, saying, Thus saith the LORD of hosts; My cities through prosperity shall yet be spread abroad; and the LORD shall yet comfort Zion, and shall yet choose Jerusalem.

Isaiah 34:1-8 is a passage that is prophetic of the Lord taking vengeance against the nations for their rejection of His grace during the dispensation of grace and for the judgment with which God avenges Israel.

Isaiah 34:1-8
> "[1] Come near, ye nations, to hear; and hearken, ye people: let the earth hear, and all that is therein; the world, and all things that come forth of it. [2] For the indignation of the LORD *is* upon all nations, and *his* fury upon all their armies: he hath utterly destroyed them, he hath delivered them to the slaughter. [The slaughter in view here is Armageddon.]

³ Their slain also shall be cast out, and their stink shall come up out of their carcasses, and the mountains shall be melted with their blood. [This is a reference to the blood that Revelation 14:20 speaks of.] ⁴ And all the host of heaven shall be dissolved, and the heavens shall be rolled together as a scroll: and all their host shall fall down, as the leaf falleth off from the vine, and as a falling *fig* from the fig tree. [This reference to the hosts of heaven falling is connected with Revelation 12 and the war in heaven.]

⁵ For my sword shall be bathed in heaven: behold, it shall come down upon Idumea, and upon the people of my curse, to judgment. [After Satan is expelled from heaven in Revelation chapter 12, the Lord comes down to earth to Edom to fight against the armies of the earth.]

⁶ The sword of the LORD is filled with blood, it is made fat with fatness, *and* with the blood of lambs and goats, with the fat of the kidneys of rams: for the LORD hath a sacrifice in Bozrah, and a great slaughter in the land of Idumea. [Bozrah is a town in Edom southeast of the Dead Sea] ⁷ And the unicorns shall come down with them, and the bullocks with the bulls; and their land shall be soaked with blood, and their dust made fat with fatness. ⁸ For *it is* the day of the LORD'S vengeance, *and* the year of recompences for the controversy of Zion. [This takes place in "The Day of the Lord"]

Isaiah 63:1-6 is a passage that describes the route that the Lord takes when He returns to the earth to begin His conquest of planet earth and the suppression of the rebellion that the nations have had against Him since the fall of man.

Isaiah 63:1-6

"¹ Who *is* this that cometh from Edom, with dyed garments from Bozrah? this *that is* glorious in his apparel, travelling in the greatness of his strength? I that speak in righteousness, mighty to save. [The dye here is the blood stains on the Lord's apparel that Revelation 14:20 speaks of when He treads the winepress of His wrath.] ² Wherefore *art thou* red in thine apparel, and thy garments like him that treadeth in the winefat? ³ I have trodden the winepress alone; and of the people *there was* none with me: for I will tread them in mine anger, and trample them in my fury; and their blood shall be sprinkled upon my garments, and I will stain all my raiment. [He comes with a great company of angels but He in His wrath is doing essentially all of the fighting.] ⁴ For the day of vengeance *is* in mine heart, and the year of my redeemed is come. [The dispensation of God's wonderful grace is over at this point in time and the world in the Day of the Lord"] ⁵ And I looked, and *there was* none to help; and I wondered that *there was* none to uphold: therefore mine own arm brought salvation unto me; and my fury, it upheld me. ⁶ And I will tread down the people in mine anger, and make them drunk in my fury, and I will bring down their strength to the earth. [The Lord came to earth the first time as a lamb to go to Calvary to accomplish redemption for all who will trust Him as Savior. He comes here the second time as the Lion of the Tribe of Judea to Conquer.]

Revelation Chapter 14 Study Guide Questions

1. Who are the 144,000 in verse 1?

2. In what sense were the 144,000 not defiled with women?

3. Paul said in Galatians 1:8 that if any preach a different gospel than what Paul preached he should be accursed. Yet here in verse 6 we see an angel preach a different gospel that Paul preached and was not accursed. How do we understand this?

4. Verse 8 preaches the fall of Babylon as predicted in Jeremiah 50 and 51 and once fallen it will never be destroyed. How do we know this has not happened already?

5. What is the warning of the third angel in verse 9?

6. Verse 16 talks about the harvest of the earth. In what way was the earth reaped?

7. How does the parable of the sower in Matthew 13:33-43 relate to this harvest of the earth?

CHAPTER 15

The seven Angels with the Seven Last Plagues

Revelation 15:1-2

"¹ And I saw another sign in heaven, great and marvellous, seven angels having the seven last plagues; for in them is filled up the wrath of God. ² And I saw as it were a sea of glass mingled with fire: and them that had gotten the victory over the beast, and over his image, and over his mark, *and* over the number of his name, stand on the sea of glass, having the harps of God." (Rev. 15:1-2)

This is taking place in heaven. They are standing on the face of the universe. Note Job 38:30 "...the face of the deep is frozen..." They are in the third heaven (2Cor. 12:3). In Genesis 1:1 there was only one heaven. When sin entered God's creation, God moved outside of His created universe and developed a plan to reconcile it back to Himself. That plan had two components – the mystery revealed through Paul would reconcile the heavens to Himself while the prophetic program concerning Israel and the Kingdom of Heaven set up on the Earth would reconcile the earth to Christ.

The Saints sing Two Songs in Heaven

Revelation 15:3-4

"³ And they sing the song of Moses the servant of God, and the song of the Lamb, saying, Great and marvelous *are* thy works, Lord God Almighty; just and true *are* thy ways, thou King of saints. ⁴ Who shall not fear thee, O Lord, and glorify thy name? for *thou* only *art* holy: for all nations shall come and worship before thee; for thy judgments are made manifest." (Rev. 15:3-4)

They sing two songs. The song of Moses is a song of victory. Moses sang it when Israel had crossed the Red Sea in Exodus 15. The song of Moses pictures the Lord as "...a man of war..." (Exod. 15:3). It portrays the horse and rider being cast into the sea (Exod. 15:1). In the Tribulation Period, the horses of Revelation 4 and its rider will be destroyed. Moses brought victory to Israel but not redemption. Therefore, the song of the Lamb is also sung by these tribulation saints as a song that brings redemption to the nation.

Seven Angels with Seven Golden Vials bring the Seven last Plagues

Revelation 15:5-8

"5 And after that I looked, and, behold, the temple of the tabernacle of the testimony in heaven was opened: 6 And the seven angels came out of the temple, having the seven plagues, clothed in pure and white linen, and having their breasts girded with golden girdles. 7 And one of the four beasts gave unto the seven angels seven golden vials full of the wrath of God, who liveth for ever and ever. 8 And the temple was filled with smoke from the glory of God, and from his power; and no man was able to enter into the temple, till the seven plagues of the seven angels were fulfilled." (Rev. 15:5-8)

The temple here is the real temple in heaven. The temple on earth was made in its likeness. (Heb. 8:5) Seven angels come out of the temple to bring the seven last plagues upon the earth to fill up the wrath of God. One of the cherubs gives the seven vials that contain the seven last plagues to the seven angels.

Revelation Chapter 15 Study Guide Questions

1. What verse in Job does the sea of glass in verse 2 remind you of?

2. What two songs do the saints sing in verse 3? What is the message of each of these songs concerning Christ?

3. What was given to the seven angels in verse 7?

4. According to Verse 1, what will these seven last plagues do?

CHAPTER 16

The angels pour out their bowls of wrath

In Chapter 15 we saw the seven angels who have the seven last plagues. These will fill up the wrath of God on those that take the mark of the beast. These plagues will be poured out after 3.5 years of famine, drought, and many other supernatural disasters that come upon the earth. Of the seven plagues in this chapter, a number of them are similar to the plagues that came upon Egypt in the Exodus. Isaiah 11:16 states that there will be a similitude between the exodus from Egypt and the entering into the Kingdom. The next three chapters could be titled as:

Chapter 16   The Great Judgment
Chapter 17   The Great Whore
Chapter 18   The Great City

The first Vial

Revelation 16:1-2

> "¹ And I heard a great voice out of the temple saying to the seven angels, Go your ways, and pour out the vials of the wrath of God upon the earth. ² And the first went, and poured out his vial upon the earth; and there fell a noisome and grievous sore upon the men which had the mark of the beast, and *upon* them which worshipped his image." (Rev. 16:1 & 2)

Those who take the mark of the beast will have a skin disease like what Moses called "the botch of Egypt" (Deut. 28:27).

The Second Vial

Revelation 16:3

> "³ And the second angel poured out his vial upon the sea; and it became as the blood of a dead *man*: and every living soul died in the sea." (Rev. 16:3)

Note that it says the sea – not the seas. This is probably a reference to the Mediterranean Sea. Most of the events of Chapters 16 through 18 are involved with the Middle East. The judgments are targeted primarily on the antichrist's kingdom. This vial is a plague parallel to Exodus 7:19. Note in Exodus. 8:22 & 23 that there was a separation between the Hebrews and the Egyptians and that the Hebrew people were spared from the curse of the flies after having endured the first two judgments along with the Egyptians. .

The Third Vial Judgment

Revelation 16:4-7

> "⁴ And the third angel poured out his vial upon the rivers and fountains of waters; and they became blood. ⁵ And I heard the angel of the waters say, Thou art righteous, O Lord, which art, and wast, and shalt be, because thou hast judged thus. ⁶ For they have shed the blood of saints and prophets, and thou hast given them blood to drink; for they are worthy. ⁷ And I heard another out of the altar say, Even so, Lord God Almighty, true and righteous *are* thy judgments." (Rev. 16:4-7)

Here the rivers and the fresh water supply become as blood. God forbad the consuming of blood: before the Law (Gen. 9:4), under the Law (Lev. 17:10), and after the Law (Acts 15: 20). The reason given for the justice in this judgment is the shed blood of the martyrs. (cf. Matt. 23:30 - 31)

The Fourth Vial Judgment

Revelation 16:8-9

> "8 And the fourth angel poured out his vial upon the sun; and power was given unto him to scorch men with fire. 9 And men were scorched with great heat, and blasphemed the name of God, which hath power over these plagues: and they repented not to give him glory." (Rev. 16: 8-9)

Isaiah 30:26 speaks of a day when the moon eill be as bright as the sun and the sun being sevenfold times brighter than normal in the day of the Lord. "Moreover the light of the moon shall be as the light of the sun, and the light of the sun shall be sevenfold, as the light of seven days, in the day that the LORD bindeth up the breach of his people, and healeth the stroke of their wound."

The Fifth Vial Judgment

Revelation 16:10-11

> "10 And the fifth angel poured out his vial upon the seat of the beast; and his kingdom was full of darkness; and they gnawed their tongues for pain, 11 And blasphemed the God of heaven because of their pains and their sores, and repented not of their deeds." (Rev. 16:10-11)

Here the judgment is on the antichrist's kingdom. This is as in Exodus 10:21 where the darkness was only on Pharaoh's kingdom. How stubborn is the unrepentant heart that it will not repent in spite of clear revelation of the power of God. The goodness of God should lead men to repentance but often instead they just "…store up unto themselves wrath against the day of wrath and the revelation of the righteous judgment of God" (Rom. 2:2-5).

The Sixth Vial Judgment

Revelation 16:12-16

> "12 And the sixth angel poured out his vial upon the great river Euphrates; and the water thereof was dried up, that the way of the kings of the east might be prepared. 13 And I saw three unclean spirits like frogs *come* out of the mouth of the dragon, and out of the mouth of the beast, and out of the mouth of the false prophet. 14 For they are the spirits of devils, working miracles, *which* go forth unto the kings of the earth and of the whole world, to gather them to the battle of that great day of God Almighty. 15 Behold, I come as a thief. Blessed *is* he that watcheth, and keepeth his garments, lest he walk naked, and they see his shame. 16 And he gathered them together into a place called in the Hebrew tongue Armageddon." (Rev. 16:12-16)

The River Euphrates is the eastern border of the area that the Bible calls Eden. Here the River Euphrates is dried up to make way for the kings of the east to invade Palestine. To the east of the Euphrates River would be Iraq and Iran (the lands of the ancient Babylonian and Persian Empires) along with the Stan countries (including Afghanistan and Pakistan) and of course India and China.

Here in verse 13 we see demons that go into the nations of the earth to convince the nations to join the antichrist in fighting against Christ to prevent Him from reclaiming what is rightfully His by right of creation and we add; by right of redemption. These are the spirits of devils working miracles. There will be real signs and wonders of Satanic origin that will be so convincing that it could almost deceive even the believers who will have the knowledge of God (1John 4:2 - 3; 2John 1:7) The antichrist will come with power and signs and lying wonders (2Thess. 2;8-10). People who want truth will find the truth but people who want to believe a lie will find a lie to believe. 1Kings 22:8ff is a case in point. God allowed Ahab to have the lie he wanted and it cost Ahab his life. This gathering in Revelation 16:16 is the calling of the armies of the earth to the Battle of Armageddon.

The term "the almighty" (vs. 13) is used a number of times in the Revelation. Jesus Christ is referred to as the Almighty in Revelation 11:17 - "Lord God Almighty, which art, and wast, and art to come..." The Father is referred to as Lord God Almighty in Revelation 4:8 and again in Revelation 21:22.

Armageddon is a place in Israel where the great battle between Christ and the antichrist will be fought. There were other battles fought there in the past. Barak under the influence and encouragement of Deborah gained a victory over Jabin King of Hazor there. (Judges 4) King Josiah died as result of wounds received in a battle there against Pharaoh Necho (2Kings 23:29; 2Chr. 35:22-24). If this is associated with the Plain of Megiddo then it is located about 9 miles west of Jezreel.

The seventh angel pours out his bowl into the air
Revelation 16:17-21

> "17 And the seventh angel poured out his vial into the air; and there came a great voice out of the temple of heaven, from the throne, saying, It is done. 18 And there were voices, and thunders, and lightnings; and there was a great earthquake, such as was not since men were upon the earth, so mighty an earthquake, *and* so great. 19 And the great city was divided into three parts, and the cities of the nations fell: and great Babylon came in remembrance before God, to give unto her the cup of the wine of the fierceness of his wrath. 20 And every island fled away, and the mountains were not found. 21 And there fell upon men a great hail out of heaven, *every stone* about the weight of a talent: and men blasphemed God because of the plague of the hail; for the plague thereof was exceeding great." (Rev. 16:17-21)

There are many prophetic passages about a shaking of the earth associated with the fall of Satan's kingdom and the time of the Lord's wrath (Isa. 2:21; 13:13; 24:18; Ezek. 31:16; Joel 3:16; Haggai 2:6, 21; Luke 21:26). This shaking of the earth will be truly cataclysmic. It will be the worst in human history. It may be that the shaking between Verses 1 and 2 of Genesis 1was worse but there was no man to see it (Jer. 4:22-25).

Let's consider the effect of the earth quake that Revelation 16:17-21 describes:
- The cities of the nations fell
- The islands of the seas disappeared
- The mountains subsided
- Hailstones of a talent in weight fell on men. A Talent is about 57 pounds in English units.

This is the taking down of the Gentile cities and cultures to make room for the culture of the Kingdom. The great city (Babylon- Rev. 14:8; 16:19; 18:10, 16, 18, 19, 21) is divided into three parts.

Revelation Chapter 16 Study Guide Questions

1. Chapter 16 contains the seven vial judgments. Summarize them and note the occurrence of blasphemy and repentance or lack thereof:

- The first vial in Verses 1-2
- The second vial in Verse 3—what sea is this talking about?
- The third vial in Verses 4-7
- The fourth vial in Verses 8-9
- The fifth vial in Verses 10-11
- The sixth vial in Verses 12-16 - This vial is doing something to set the stage for the battle of Armageddon. What is it that sets the stage? What countries are east of the Euphrates?
- The seventh Vial in Verses 17-21-- List four calamities that come upon the earth as a result of this via

CHAPTER 17

A woman arrayed in purple and scarlet, with a golden cup in her hand, sits on a scarlet beast

Revelation 17:1-6

> "¹ And there came one of the seven angels which had the seven vials, and talked with me, saying unto me, Come hither; I will shew unto thee the judgment of the great whore that sitteth upon many waters: ² With whom the kings of the earth have committed fornication, and the inhabitants of the earth have been made drunk with the wine of her fornication. ³ So he carried me away in the spirit into the wilderness: and I saw a woman sit upon a scarlet coloured beast, full of names of blasphemy, having seven heads and ten horns. ⁴ And the woman was arrayed in purple and scarlet colour, and decked with gold and precious stones and pearls, having a golden cup in her hand full of abominations and filthiness of her fornication: ⁵ And upon her forehead *was* a name written, MYSTERY, BABYLON THE GREAT, THE MOTHER OF HARLOTS AND ABOMINATIONS OF THE EARTH. ⁶ And I saw the woman drunken with the blood of the saints, and with the blood of the martyrs of Jesus: and when I saw her, I wondered with great admiration." (Rev. 17:1-6)

There is much to study and figure out in this passage. Who is the woman? What is the significance of her name? Who or what is the beast on which she rides and why does he carry the woman? Who or what do the ten horns represent? What is the significance of the seven heads?

First let's consider and identify the woman. The woman's name is Mystery Babylon the Great, the Mother of Harlots and the Abominations of the Earth. The name "Mystery" means that one has to study Scripture to understand who she is. Also, her form changes with time. The name "Babylon the Great" describes her origin. The name "Mother of Harlots and Abominations of the Earth" describes her activity. She is a city. Verse 18 tells us that she is that great city that reigns over the kings of the earth. Revelation 18:10 tells us that Babylon is that great city. Babylon will have to be rebuilt before this final destruction can happen. Religious systems have cities as headquarters:

- Judaism is headquartered in Jerusalem
- Islam is headquartered in Mecca
- Apostate Christianity is headquartered in Rome
- The Great Whore is headquartered in Babylon

In the Bible whoredom and fornication is associated with idolatry. Just as sexual fornication takes what rightly belongs to one man and gives it to another who has no right to it, so spiritual fornication takes the worship that rightly belongs to God and gives it to another. This woman is a system of idolatry associated with the city of Babylon. Babylon first appears in Scripture as the city that Nimrod built in defiance of God (Gen. 10:10). It is there that idolatry started as a means to keep people away from the true God. It was the founding of Babel that resulted in the Gentiles nations being scattered and set aside by God (Rom. 1:21ff). It was with the building of Babel and the tower there that man set out to exclude God from God's creation and to worship the creature rather that he creator. Babel was:

- a religious system (represented by the tower),
- an economic system (represented by Nimrod being a mighty hunter before the Lord),
- And it was a political system (represented by the city and the name).

The idolatry has to do with the religious system and is what is primarily in view here in Revelation 17. However, it is apparent that the woman is also associated with an economic system and a political system as seen by how the kings of the earth mourn after her destruction (Rev. 18:11-19). The political rulers of the earth are intoxicated with the same idolatry that the woman promotes – of denying God the worship due to Him. The idolatry of today is largely humanism, atheism and agnosticism as time and chance are worshipped as the creator of all things and humans are left as the final authority. Though this system has changed form through time since its origin at Babel, the goal of the system is to deny God the privilege of enjoying His creation. Babel was founded as a symbol of rebellion against God when men rejected God's command to spread across the face of the earth in Genesis 10. The heart attitude that produced Babylon is seen in Psalm 2: 2-3 "2 The kings of the earth set themselves, and the rulers take counsel together, against the LORD, and against his anointed, *saying*, 3 Let us break their bands asunder, and cast away their cords from us."

Let's summarize what we know of the woman of Revelation 17:
- She sits on many waters. The waters on which the woman sits are peoples and multitudes, and nations and tongues (Verse 15). From this we understand that the system is all over the world. (Verse 1)
- The political leaders of the earth and the inhabitants have joined in on her idolatry whereby they deny God the worship due Him. (Verse 2)
- The beast carried her and supported her for a time. (Verse 3). The beast (the antichrist) uses her to gain control over the kings of the earth.
- She is treated as royalty as seen by the purple and scarlet of her apparel and is rich in material wealth (Verse 4).
- The golden cup in her hand is the symbol of Babylon (Jer. 51:6-8).
- This system is responsible for the martyrdom of many of the saints of the Lord (Verse 6).

The Identities of the Woman and the Beast Revealed

Revelation 17:7-13

"7 And the angel said unto me, Wherefore didst thou marvel? I will tell thee the mystery of the woman, and of the beast that carrieth her, which hath the seven heads and ten horns. 8 The beast that thou sawest was, and is not; and shall ascend out of the bottomless pit, and go into perdition: and they that dwell on the earth shall wonder, whose names were not written in the book of life from the foundation of the world, when they behold the beast that was, and is not, and yet is. 9 And here *is* the mind which hath wisdom. The seven heads are seven mountains, on which the woman sitteth. 10 And there are seven kings: five are fallen, and one is, *and* the other is not yet come; and when he cometh, he must continue a short space. 11 And the beast that was, and is not, even he is the eighth, and is of the seven, and goeth into perdition. 12 And the ten horns which thou sawest are ten kings, which have received no kingdom as yet; but receive power as kings one hour with the beast. 13 These have one mind, and shall give their power and strength unto the beast." (Rev. 17:7-13)

Just as the woman changes form through time so does the beast having seven heads and ten horns. We find this beast first in Daniel 7 and then in Revelation 12:3, 13:1, and here in Chapter 17. The seven heads are seven mountains. Mountains in Scripture represent kingdoms (Isa. 2:2; Amos 6:1; Mic. 4:1-2; etc.). These are seven kingdoms that held reign over Israel and seven kings. Five are fallen, one is, and the other is not yet come at the writing of this by John (Verse 10). These are seven nations that speak against and oppressed God's nation of Israel. Five that are fallen are: Egypt, Assyria, Babylon, Media-Persia, and Greece. The one that "is" (at the writing of the Revelation) was Rome. The one that is to come is the kingdom of the antichrist (the man of sin). He is also the eighth (the son of perdition). Note how Satan counterfeits Christ. The beast was and is not and shall ascend out of the bottomless pit (Verse 8). Christ "is, was, and is to come (Rev. 1:8). The beast is the man of sin for the first part (the first half) of the 7 years (the seventieth week of Daniel Chapter 9) and then dies (Zech. 11:17) and appears to rise again (Rev. 13:3 & 12). He then (after his deadly wound is healed) becomes the son of Perdition in the second half of the seventieth week (2Thess. 2:3). Interestingly, Judas is referred to as the son of perdition (John 17:12). Also, Judas Iscariot went to a unique place (Acts 1:25). The antichrist comes from a unique place (Rev. 11:17; 17:8). Both are referred to as a devil (John 6:20 and Rev. 2:10).

The ten horns on the beast are ten kings that shall receive power with the beast for one hour. This reference to one hour is figurative. Revelation 14:7 speaks of the hour of God's judgment as covering 3.5 years. So too these ten kings receive power with the beast for 3.5 years (the second half of the seventieth week). The ten horns of Revelation 17 correspond with the ten toes of Daniel 2:41 and the ten horns of Daniel 7:7. The ten horns are ten kings that come up in the Mediterranean area. These hate the woman and seek to destroy her. These kings are demonic (Dan. 2:43). Their goal is to direct all worship to the antichrist who comes in his own name to receive the worship of the people of the earth (John 5:43). The antichrist uses the religious system (which the woman actually is) to gain influence over the kings of the earth. At that point, the religious system of Babylon (represented by the woman) will be no longer of use to the beast. In Psalm 83 we find mention of ten nations that desire to cut Israel off from being a nation. These take counsel against the "hidden ones." This (the hidden ones) is probably a reference to the children of Israel during the Tribulation period when they flee into the wilderness to be protected from destruction by the antichrist (Rev. 12:8). The nations of Psalm 83 are peoples of the Middle East in the area surrounding Israel today. These do not exist or are difficult to identify as nations today. However, they are today all Islamic peoples. We can expect that when the end times come that these will be nations and will indeed be confederate with the antichrist against Israel.

The victory of the Lamb
Revelation 17:14-18

> "14 These shall make war with the Lamb, and the Lamb shall overcome them: for he is Lord of lords, and King of kings: and they that are with him *are* called, and chosen, and faithful. 15 And he saith unto me, The waters which thou sawest, where the whore sitteth, are peoples, and multitudes, and nations, and tongues. 16 And the ten horns which thou sawest upon the beast, these shall hate the whore, and shall make her desolate and naked, and shall eat her flesh, and burn her with fire. 17 For God hath put in their hearts to fulfil his will, and to agree, and give their kingdom unto the beast, until the words of God shall be fulfilled. 18 And the woman which thou sawest is that great city, which reigneth over the kings of the earth." (Rev. 17:14-18)

The antichrist and the ten nations under him will hate the whore because he desires to be worshipped above all that is called God or that is worshipped (2Thess. 2:4). The woman is a city called "that great city." Babylon is called "that great city" in Revelation 14:8; 16:19; 18:10, 21). One day Babylon will apparently be rebuilt as a center of commerce and political power and the home of an idolatrous religious system which will actually worship Satan.

Revelation Chapter 17 Study Guide Questions

1. Who is the woman in verse 1?

2. What is the significance of her name?

3. Who or what is the beast on which she rides?

4. Why does he carry the woman?

5. Who or what do the ten horns represent?

6. What is the significance of the seven heads? What nations do they represent?

7. What does the description of the beast as he "...was, and is not, and shall ascend out of the bottomless pit..." mean?

8. What does it mean "...and shall go into perdition..."?

9. What does the term "many waters" mean in Verse 1 and 15?

10. Compare Verse 18 with Revelation 14:8; 16:19; and 18:10 & 21 and identify who the woman is.

CHAPTER 18

Babylon falls

Revelation 18:1-3

> "¹ And after these things I saw another angel come down from heaven, having great power; and the earth was lightened with his glory. ² And he cried mightily with a strong voice, saying, Babylon the great is fallen, is fallen, and is become the habitation of devils, and the hold of every foul spirit, and a cage of every unclean and hateful bird. ³ For all nations have drunk of the wine of the wrath of her fornication, and the kings of the earth have committed fornication with her, and the merchants of the earth are waxed rich through the abundance of her delicacies." (Rev. 18:1-3)

The site of where Babylon is will become the "hold" and "cage" (as in a type of prison) for "...every foul spirit and a cage of every unclean and hateful bird". These are demonic creatures. These will be held there in prison during the millennium.

This reference to "every unclean and hateful bird" is an interesting term. The birds that we know are not what can be considered a hateful bird. Let's consider this passage in light of Jeremiah 4:23-26 "I beheld the earth, and, lo, *it was* without form, and void; and the heavens, and they *had* no light. I beheld the mountains, and, lo, they trembled, and all the hills moved lightly. I beheld, and, lo, *there was* no man, and all the birds of the heavens were fled. I beheld, and, lo, the fruitful place *was* a wilderness, and all the cities thereof were broken down at the presence of the LORD, *and* by his fierce anger." Now consider this passage in Jeremiah in light of Genesis 1:2 and note the similarity. Note also that the commission given to Adam was that he was to replenish the earth (Genesis 1:28). This leads us to ask "who populated the earth before Adam?" but who then left it (or was removed from it)? We note also that the first step in Lucifer's five point plan of rebellion was that he would ascend into heaven. We understand then that he was not supposed to be in heaven for it was rebellion for him to desire to ascend to it. The fact that Lucifer before his fall was "the anointed cherub that covereth [i.e. that covered the throne of God]." (Ezekiel 28:14) We noted in Revelation 12:4 that one third of the angelic host followed Lucifer in rebellion. These then would be the winged creature (fallen cherubim and seraphim) who comprise the unclean and hateful birds of Jeremiah 4:25 and the group that are held in the cage that Revelation 18:2 talks about.

Verse 3 brings three indictments against Babylon:

1. The nations are drunk with the wine of wrath of her fornication. Fornication is the use of something that has a holy and honorable purpose but which is used for selfish pleasures as in sexual fornication. However, this is fornication that nations commit. The fornication in view here is more of a spiritual nature. This would be governments using that which should be bringing joy to God and using it for self aggrandizement. This is governments drawing people away from pursuit of God to pursuit of its own profit.

2. The kings of the earth have committed fornication with her. Here again the fornication is of a spiritual nature whereby political gain is made by drawing people away form God. The Political leaders of the earth have used the Babylonian system to gain power and influence by means of graft and corruption to maximize personal profits instead of seeking the mutual benefit for all parties.

3. The merchants of the earth have waxed rich through the abundance of her delicacies. These are not manufacturers of goods but those who petal the goods that are made. This would be the promoting of the

desire for conspicuous consumption that brings personal wealth to the merchants while diverting people away from the God centered activities of marriage and family.

The judgment on Babylon

Revelation 18:4-8

"4 And I heard another voice from heaven, saying, Come out of her, my people, that ye be not partakers of her sins, and that ye receive not of her plagues. 5 For her sins have reached unto heaven, and God hath remembered her iniquities. 6 Reward her even as she rewarded you, and double unto her double according to her works: in the cup which she hath filled fill to her double. 7 How much she hath glorified herself, and lived deliciously, so much torment and sorrow give her: for she saith in her heart, I sit a queen, and am no widow, and shall see no sorrow. 8 Therefore shall her plagues come in one day, death, and mourning, and famine; and she shall be utterly burned with fire: for strong *is* the Lord God who judgeth her." (Rev. 18:4-8)

This woman is a queen (the queen of heaven of Jeremiah 7:18; 44:17,-19, 25). She has a husband (Satan). The house that will be built in the land of Shinar (Zechariah 5:11) is probably this woman. Isaiah 47:1-15 talks about the destruction (by fire) of the woman who is called the Lady of Kingdoms. This Babylon the great of Verse 2 is the uniting of religious Babylon with political and commercial Babylon.

The Merchants of the Earth Mourn the Fall of Babylon

Revelation 18:9-11

"9 And the kings of the earth, who have committed fornication and lived deliciously with her, shall bewail her, and lament for her, when they shall see the smoke of her burning, 10 Standing afar off for the fear of her torment, saying, Alas, alas, that great city Babylon, that mighty city! for in one hour is thy judgment come. 11 And the merchants of the earth shall weep and mourn over her; for no man buyeth their merchandise any more: (Rev. 18:9-11)

Verse 10 and Verse 17 speaks of the destruction of Babylon being so fast that it is essentially in one hour. One can't help but to think of the destruction of Sodom and Gomorra in reading this.

Revelation 18:12-19

12 The merchandise of gold, and silver, and precious stones, and of pearls, and fine linen, and purple, and silk, and scarlet, and all thyine wood, and all manner vessels of ivory, and all manner vessels of most precious wood, and of brass, and iron, and marble, 13 And cinnamon, and odours, and ointments, and frankincense, and wine, and oil, and fine flour, and wheat, and beasts, and sheep, and horses, and chariots, and slaves, and souls of men. 14 And the fruits that thy soul lusted after are departed from thee, and all things which were dainty and goodly are departed from thee, and thou shalt find them no more at all. 15 The merchants of these things, which were made rich by her, shall stand afar off for the fear of her torment, weeping and wailing, 16 And saying, Alas, alas, that great city, that was clothed in fine linen, and purple, and scarlet, and decked with gold, and precious stones, and pearls. 17 For in one hour so great riches is come to nought. And every shipmaster, and all the company in ships, and sailors, and as many as trade by sea, stood afar off, 18 And cried when they saw the smoke of her burning, saying, What *city is* like unto this great city. 19 And they cast dust on their heads, and cried, weeping and wailing, saying, Alas, alas, that great city,

wherein were made rich all that had ships in the sea by reason of her costliness! for in one hour is she made desolate. (Rev. 18:12-19)

In Verses 12 through 13 we see the nature of her merchandise. This is what men today consider the finer things in life. But notice that in Verse 13 slaves and the souls of men are included in the merchandise that is trafficked. Souls can be trafficked by physical means for sexual purposes or by religious means whereby souls are taken captive by religious systems that hold men in religious bondage.

Note also in verse 17 "And every shipmaster, and all the company in ships, and sailors, and as many as trade by sea, stood afar off…" are the mourners over the loss of Babylon. This speaks of international maritime commerce much like the merchant marine that we observe coming to American ports on a daily basis today.

The Saints rejoiced over that over which the merchants mourned

Revelation 18:20-24

> [20] Rejoice over her, *thou* heaven, and *ye* holy apostles and prophets; for God hath avenged you on her. [21] And a mighty angel took up a stone like a great millstone, and cast *it* into the sea, saying, Thus with violence shall that great city Babylon be thrown down, and shall be found no more at all. [22] And the voice of harpers, and musicians, and of pipers, and trumpeters, shall be heard no more at all in thee; and no craftsman, of whatsoever craft *he be*, shall be found any more in thee; and the sound of a millstone shall be heard no more at all in thee; [23] And the light of a candle shall shine no more at all in thee; and the voice of the bridegroom and of the bride shall be heard no more at all in thee: for thy merchants were the great men of the earth; for by thy sorceries were all nations deceived. [24] And in her was found the blood of prophets, and of saints, and of all that were slain upon the earth." (Rev. 18:20-24)

The kings of the earth and the merchants who became rich through her mourn for her (Verses 15 thru 19) but there are others that rejoice over her destruction (Verses 20 thru 24). The heavens, the apostles, and the prophets rejoice for the vengeance that God took on her for the blood that she shed of the martyrs. Remember that this is the political, economic, religious system that united the masses of humanity at Babel (Gen. 11:4) and has ever since sought to exclude God from His creation. This is the system responsible for the persecution of those (the apostles and prophets) who sought to direct man to the worship of the true God.

Verse 21 speaks of the overthrow of Babylon by a violent means. This too brings our thoughts back to the destruction of Sodom by some nuclear means.

Verse 22 implies that the city is known for a highly cultured society. This would lead one to think in terms of Hollywood's personal self aggrandizement of itself while flaunting open sin and ungodliness. In Verse 23 we see that Babylon used sorceries to deceive the nations. This speaks of witchcraft and drug use for the purpose of captivating people of the nations. Note that here merchants were the great men of the earth (verse 23).

Revelation Chapter 18 Study Guide Questions

1. Verse 2 describes the future use that will be made of the site that Babylon presently occupies. What will that use be?

2. In Verse 7 we see that Babylon considered herself a queen. What other Old Testament passage might refer to one who is called a queen in a religious sense?

3. Verse 9 suggests that the kings of the earth have committed fornication with Babylon. What kind of fornication would this be?

4. Verse 11 says that the merchant of the earth mourn over the destruction of Babylon. Why would this be?

5. Verses 12 – 16 list the merchandise of Babylon. Do we see such merchandise in Babylon today? What does this suggest about the future of that city between now and its final destruction?

6. Verse 10, 17 and 19 talks about the suddenness of the destruction. Can you think of two cities in Genesis that suffered similar destruction?

7. Who rejoiced over Babylon's destruction in Verse 20?

8. According to Verse 21, what kind of destruction is in store for Babylon?

9. Verses 22 and 23 talks about the culture of Babylon. How would you describe it?

10. According to Verse 23, what did the merchants of Babylon use to deceive people?

11. Verses 20 and 24 indicate that the city was responsible for what?

CHAPTER 19

The Alleluia Chorus

Revelation 19:1-3

"¹ And after these things I heard a great voice of much people in heaven, saying, Alleluia; Salvation, and glory, and honour, and power, unto the Lord our God: ² For true and righteous *are* his judgments: for he hath judged the great whore, which did corrupt the earth with her fornication, and hath avenged the blood of his servants at her hand. ³ And again they said, Alleluia. And her smoke rose up for ever and ever. ⁴ And the four and twenty elders and the four beasts fell down and worshipped God that sat on the throne, saying, Amen; Alleluia. ⁵ And a voice came out of the throne, saying, Praise our God, all ye his servants, and ye that fear him, both small and great." (Rev. 19:1-3)

The term "Alleluia" is used over 20 times in the Old Testament. The only place that it is used in the New Testament is here in Revelation 19. The term means "Praise the Lord." It is used wherever judgment is poured out on God's enemies. Here we see much praising at the destruction of the city of man (man's city). It is at the destruction of this city of man that we see the City of God come into the picture. The city of man (Babylon) has a husband (Satan). So too, the City of God has a husband – that being Christ.

The Bride

Revelation 19:6-8

"⁶ And I heard as it were the voice of a great multitude, and as the voice of many waters, and as the voice of mighty thunderings, saying, Alleluia: for the Lord God omnipotent reigneth. ⁷ Let us be glad and rejoice, and give honour to him: for the marriage of the Lamb is come, and his wife hath made herself ready. ⁸ And to her was granted that she should be arrayed in fine linen, clean and white: for the fine linen is the righteousness of saints." (Rev. 19:6-8)

Going back to Revelation 3:4 and 5 we see who these are that comprise the bride. This bride is the believing over comers of Israel that come through the Tribulation period. It is important to note that not all of Israel is included in the bride. Note from John 3:29 we see that John the Baptizer does not regard himself as a member of the bride. Also, note from Matthew 9:14 and 15 that the disciples are not included in the bride. The over comers that chapters 2 and 3 talk about are the over comers of the tribulation period and comprise the bride of Revelation 21:7.

The Marriage of the Lamb

Revelation 19:9-10 "⁹ And he saith unto me, Write, Blessed *are* they which are called unto the marriage supper of the Lamb. And he saith unto me, These are the true sayings of God. ¹⁰ And I fell at his feet to worship him. And he said unto me, See *thou do it* not: I am thy fellowservant, and of thy brethren that have the testimony of Jesus: worship God: for the testimony of Jesus is the spirit of prophecy." (Rev. 19:9-10)

Who is the bride? There are some Pauline passages (e.g. 2Cor. 11:1; Eph. 5:21; Rom. 7:4, etc.) that would lead people to think that the Church which is Christ's Body would be the bride. However, we today are members of the Bride groom – members of Christ. We are in special relationship that is referred to as "the preaching of Jesus Christ according to the revelation of the mystery..." (See Romans 16:25 and Ephesians 3:1-12) today. Ephesians 5 uses marriage to illustrate that we are one flesh with Christ. However, the bride here is a city as we will see in Chapter 21.   Isaiah 62:2ff says of Israel "And the Gentiles shall see thy righteousness, and all kings thy glory: and thou shalt be called by a new name, which the mouth of the LORD shall name.... Thou shalt no more be termed Forsaken; neither shall thy land any more be termed Desolate: but thou shalt be called Hephzibah ["my delight is in her"], and thy land Beulah ["married"]: for the LORD delighteth in thee, and thy land shall be married...and as the bridegroom rejoices over the bride, so shall thy God rejoice over thee." Israel committed adultery and therefore God "put her away" (Jer. 3:8). God was Israel's Husband (Jer. 31:31) but Israel departed from the relationship. To get Israel to understand what she did to her husband, God had Hosea marry the whore Gomer (Hos. 1:2). But God tells Israel that He will take her back (Hos. 2:18ff). Revelation 19:17 is the marriage whereby God does so. Israel will be married to the land, and Christ will be married to both the nation and the land.

Jesus Christ Revealed in Glory

Revelation 19:11-13

"[11] And I saw heaven opened, and behold a white horse; and he that sat upon him *was* called Faithful and True, and in righteousness he doth judge and make war. [12] His eyes *were* as a flame of fire, and on his head *were* many crowns; and he had a name written, that no man knew, but he himself. [13] And he *was* clothed with a vesture dipped in blood: and his name is called The Word of God." (Rev.19:11-13)

We saw the reign of Christ begin in Heaven in Chapter 12. Here we see him begin to establish His reign on the earth as He prepares to judge and make war. His name in Verse 13 is "The Word of God." This is significant. He is the eternal Word in John 1:1-4 by whom everything that was made had been made. He is the eternal creator. What is happening here in the Revelation is that He is now returning to the earth to claim what is His by right of Creation. All of the redeemed of the ages are His by right of redemption. The fact that Verse 12 mentions that he has a name written that nobody knew but Himself takes us back to such passages as Judges 13:17 and 22 where God tells Manoah that His name is a secret.

He Returns to Judge

Revelation 19:14-15

"[14] And the armies *which were* in heaven followed him upon white horses, clothed in fine linen, white and clean. [15] And out of his mouth goeth a sharp sword, that with it he should smite the nations: and he shall rule them with a rod of iron: and he treadeth the winepress of the fierceness and wrath of Almighty God." (Rev. 19:14-15)

In Revelation 2:2 and 2:27 we saw that the faithful remnant out of the Tribulation period (the over comers) will rule with a rod of iron. This is the man child that we saw in Revelation 12:5. Here we see that it is Christ that will rule with a rod of iron. What we are observing here is that Christ will rule the earth through Israel. So too as we study Pauline passages as 2Timothy 2:12; 1Corinthians 6:3; and Colossians 1:20 we understand that Christ will rule in the heavens through the church the Body of Christ. We thus understand the twofold purpose of God. The purpose for the heavens (Ephesians 3:11) being to reconcile it to Himself through the Body of Christ and the purpose for the earth to do the same through the nation of Israel (Isa. 14:24-27; 23:9; Jer. 4:28). The twofold purpose of God in Christ is thus understood by the following verses:

1. **Regarding the earth**

Isaiah 14:24-26 "24 The LORD of hosts hath sworn, saying, Surely as I have thought, so shall it come to pass; and as I have purposed, *so* shall it stand: 25 That I will break the Assyrian in my land, and upon my mountains tread him under foot: then shall his yoke depart from off them, and his burden depart from off their shoulders. 26 This *is* the purpose that is purposed upon the whole earth: and this *is* the hand that is stretched out upon all the nations."

Isaiah 23:9 "9 The LORD of hosts hath purposed it, to stain the pride of all glory, *and* to bring into contempt all the honourable of the earth."

2. Regarding the Heavens

Ephesians 1:9-11 9 Having made known unto us the mystery of his will, according to his good pleasure which he hath purposed in himself: 10 That in the dispensation of the fulness of times he might gather together in one all things in Christ, both which are in heaven, and which are on earth; *even* in him: 11 In whom also we have obtained an inheritance, being predestinated according to the purpose of him who worketh all things after the counsel of his own will:

Ephesians 3:10-11 "10 To the intent that now unto the principalities and powers in heavenly *places* might be known by the church the manifold wisdom of God, 11 According to the eternal purpose which he purposed in Christ Jesus our Lord:"

An important question here on Verse 14 is "Who is it that comprises the armies of heaven?" There are many who hold the view that this army (or armies) is composed of the redeemed of the earth who are saved during this present dispensation of grace. The proof texts that they use are 1Thessalonians 3:13; 2Thessalonians 1:18; and Jude 1:14. We will look at each of these verses but let's first get the understanding of where the eternal destiny of the church the body of Christ will be. The Epistle of 2Corinthians 5 verse 1 clearly states that our resurrection bodies will be eternally in the heavens. God will not have us do what He has angels to do. Today during the dispensation of grace, the elect angels have a role of being students in which they learn about the wisdom of God by observing how the grace of God produces practical righteousness in us by grace (Eph. 3:10). Their role will switch back to being Israel's protectors and advocates once the dispensation of grace is closed.

The verse in 1Thessalonians 3:13 is actually talking about Jesus presenting the church the Body of Christ to the Father in Heaven. It has nothing to do with the saints of this present dispensation returning to earth for any reason.

1Thessalonians 3:11-13 "11 Now God himself and our Father, and our Lord Jesus Christ, direct our way unto you. 12 And the Lord make you to increase and abound in love one toward another, and toward all *men*, even as we *do* toward you: 13 To the end he may stablish your hearts unblameable in holiness before God, even our Father, at the coming of our Lord Jesus Christ with all his saints."

The passage in 2Thessalonians 1:10 is talking about Jesus coming to earth and also coming to His saints but it is not talking about Him coming with His saints. Note in Verse 7 that He will be revealed from heaven with His mighty angels. It is the angels that are in the armies of heaven and not men.

2 Thessalonians 1:6-10 "6 Seeing *it is* a righteous thing with God to recompense tribulation to them that trouble you; 7 And to you who are troubled rest with us, when the Lord Jesus shall be revealed from heaven with his mighty angels, 8 In flaming fire taking vengeance on them that know not God, and that obey not the gospel of our Lord Jesus Christ: 9 Who shall be punished with everlasting destruction from the presence of the Lord, and from the glory of his power; 10 When he shall come to be glorified in his saints, and to be admired in all them that believe (because our testimony among you was believed) in that day."

The passage in Jude Verse 14 is talking about Jesus Coming with His saints but the saints are the angels who are coming to earth with Him to take vengeance. The term "saints" means simply "Holy ones." There are saints in the realm of men and also in that of angels.

> **Jude 1:13-14** "[13] Raging waves of the sea, foaming out their own shame; wandering stars, to whom is reserved the blackness of darkness for ever. [14] And Enoch also, the seventh from Adam, prophesied of these, saying, Behold, the Lord cometh with ten thousands of his saints,"

King of Kings and Lord of Lords

Revelation 19:16-19

> "[16] And he hath on *his* vesture and on his thigh a name written, KING OF KINGS, AND LORD OF LORDS. [17] And I saw an angel standing in the sun; and he cried with a loud voice, saying to all the fowls that fly in the midst of heaven, Come and gather yourselves together unto the supper of the great God; [18] That ye may eat the flesh of kings, and the flesh of captains, and the flesh of mighty men, and the flesh of horses, and of them that sit on them, and the flesh of all *men, both* free and bond, both small and great. [19] And I saw the beast, and the kings of the earth, and their armies, gathered together to make war against him that sat on the horse, and against his army." (Rev. 19:16-19)

Revelation 2:7 and 3:12 spoke of a new name. Verse 16 tells us what the new name is. In Verse 17 we see a mighty angel invite the fowl of the air to scavenge the flesh of mighty men of the earth who are gathered together to fight against the Lord Jesus Christ seeking to prevent Him from taking possession of the earth that He created.

The Lake of Fire

Revelation 19:20-21

> "[20] And the beast was taken, and with him the false prophet that wrought miracles before him, with which he deceived them that had received the mark of the beast, and them that worshipped his image. These both were cast alive into a lake of fire burning with brimstone. [21] And the remnant were slain with the sword of him that sat upon the horse, which *sword* proceeded out of his mouth: and all the fowls were filled with their flesh." (Rev. 19:20-21)

This is the first reference in the Bible to the Lake of Fire. The Lake of Fire appears elsewhere by different names. It is referred to as "outer darkness" in Matthew 8:22, 22:13 and 25:30 and as "everlasting fire prepared for the devil and his angels..." in Matthew 25:41. This lake of fire was prepared originally for the devil and his angels. It was prepared by God to show the fallen angels what awaits them. We see from Matthew 8:29 that the fallen angels (devils) know what is coming. However, this Lake of Fire is currently unoccupied. Eventually, we will see in later chapters that all unsaved of humanity and all fallen angels and demons will end up there.

Revelation Chapter 19 Study Guide Questions

1. What does the term "Alleluia" mean? Why do we see it used here?

2. According to verse 10, what is the testimony of Jesus?

3. The marriage of the Lamb is mentioned in Verse 7. We saw in Revelation 3:4 & 5 who they are that comprise the bride. Who are they?

4. Who are and who are not members of the group called the "bride?" Are we who are members of the church the Body of Christ members of the bride?

5. Isaiah 62:2 and forward says that Israel shall be called by a new name. What will that new name for Israel be? What will be the new name for the land?

6. Who is riding the white horse in Revelation 19;11? What is His name? What is he coming to do?

7. In Verse 19 we find who it is that will fight against the armies in heaven. Who are they?

8. What according to Verse 20 happens to the beast and the false prophet?

A Study in the Revelation

CHAPTER 20

Satan Bound 1,000 Years

Revelation 20:1-3

"¹ And I saw an angel come down from heaven, having the key of the bottomless pit and a great chain in his hand. ² And he laid hold on the dragon, that old serpent, which is the Devil, and Satan, and bound him a thousand years, ³ And cast him into the bottomless pit, and shut him up, and set a seal upon him, that he should deceive the nations no more, till the thousand years should be fulfilled: and after that he must be loosed a little season." (Rev. 20:1-3)

The bottomless pit is at the very heart of the earth. The Pit is a term that is used for the place called Sheole (the Hebrew word for hell) in the Old Testament and Hades (Greek word for Hell) in the New Testament. Note the following passages on the subject:

Numbers 16:30 "...they go down quick into the pit..."
Numbers 16:33 "...went down alive into the pit..."
Job 17:16 "...They shall go down to the bars of the pit..."
Job 33:24 "...Deliver him from going down to the pit..."
Psalm 28:1 "...I became like them that go down to the pit..."
Psalm 30:3 "...Thou hast kept me alive, that I should not go down to the pit..."
Psalm 30:9 "...when I go down to the pit..."
Proverbs 1:12 "Let us swallow them up alive as the grave; and whole, as those that go down into the pit."
Ezekiel 31:16 "I made nations to shake at the sound of his fall, when I cast him down to hell with them that descend into the pit...all that drink water, shall be comforted in the nether parts of the earth."
Ezekiel 32:18 "... unto the nether parts of the earth, with them that go down into the pit."

Isaiah 14:15 is prophetic and talks about the antichrist's arrival into hell "Yet thou shalt be brought down to hell, to the sides of the pit." The antichrist undergoes a change in the middle of the tribulation period. Before this change he is referred to as the man of sin. After it, he is referred to as the son of perdition. The change takes place through his death and apparent resurrection. He goes to the pit as "the man of sin." However, he goes to the Lake of Fire in Revelation 19:20 as "the son of perdition." Here in Revelation 20:3 the Dragon (Satan) is bound in the bottomless pit while the false prophet and the antichrist are in the Lake of Fire. However, the Dragon's stay in the bottomless pit is only for 1,000 years.

The Millennium

Revelation 20:4

"[4] And I saw thrones, and they sat upon them, and judgment was given unto them: and *I saw* the souls of them that were beheaded for the witness of Jesus, and for the word of God, and which had not worshipped the beast, neither his image, neither had received *his* mark upon their foreheads, or in their hands; and they lived and reigned with Christ a thousand years." (Rev. 20:4)

Here we see the Man Child of Revelation 12:5 reign with Christ for 1,000 years. This is the reward to the over comers of Chapters 2 and 3. The kingdom never ends. This 1,000 year period is simply the introductory phase to the kingdom. It is only here in the Book of the Revelation that we find a reference to this 1,000 years long introductory phase to the kingdom. The Old Testament prophecies regarding the kingdom indicate that it is an eternal kingdom (Isa. 9:6). There are many prophecies about what life will be like in the kingdom. The following four pages is a summary of information contained in the book by C R Stam *"Things that Differ"* regarding what life will be like in the kingdom.

Life in the Kingdom of Heaven: There are many facts about the coming Kingdom of Heaven that we glean from the Scriptures that prophesy of it. We list a few:
- It will be set up on the earth.
- Psalms 2:8 "I shall give thee (Messiah) the… earth for thy possession"
- Isaiah 11:9 "The earth shall be full of the knowledge of the Lord"
- Jeremiah 23:5 "A king shall reign and prosper and shall execute judgment and justice in the earth."
- Isaiah 42:4 "He shall not fail nor be discouraged, till he have set judgment in the earth".
- Matthew 5:5 "Blessed are the meek, for they shall inherit the earth".
- Matthew 6:10 Thy kingdom come, Thy will be done on earth as it is in heaven. Though it is called the "kingdom of heaven" (Matt. 3:1, 2; 4:17; 10:5-7), it will be set up on the earth (Dan. 2:44).

a) It will be a theocracy on earth in which God reigns in the person of Jesus Christ.
- Isaiah 7:14 "They shall call His name Emmanuel, which being interpreted is God with us ".
- Isaiah 9:6 "His name shall be called…the mighty God"
- Zechariah 14:9 "The Lord shall be king over all the earth" (cf. vs. 16)

b) Jerusalem will be the capital city.
- Isaiah 24:23 "The Lord of hosts shall reign in Mt. Zion, and in Jerusalem".
- Isaiah 2:3 "Out of Zion shall go forth the law, and the word of the Lord from Jerusalem".
- Jeremiah 3:17 "At that time they shall call Jerusalem the throne of the Lord".
- The Lord will rule over Israel (Micah 5:2), and He will reign on the throne of David (Luke 1:32,33; cf. Matt. 2:1&2; 19:28).

c) The kingdom will extend to the entire earth through Israel.
- Psalm 72:11 "All kings shall fall down before Him; all nations shall serve Him".

- Daniel 7:14 "And there was given Him dominion, and glory, and a kingdom, that all people, nations, and languages should serve Him".
- Zechariah 8:22 "Many people and strong nations shall come to seek the Lord of hosts in Jerusalem, and to pray before the Lord."

d) All Israel shall be saved.
- Jeremiah 31:34 "They [the Redeemed of Israel] shall all know me, from the least of them unto the greatest of them".
- Ezekiel 37:23 "I will save them…and will cleanse them. So shall they be my people, and I will be their God".
- Romans 11:26 "And so all Israel shall be saved: as it is written, there shall come out of Sion the Deliverer and shall turn away ungodliness from Jacob."

e) Israel will be a blessing to the nations. This will be the fulfillment of the Abrahamic Covenant
- Isaiah 60:3 "The Gentiles shall come to thy light, and kings to the brightness of thy rising".
- Zechariah 8:13 "And it shall come to pass, that as ye were a curse among the heathen,… so will I save you, and ye shall be a blessing".
- Genesis 22:17-18 "In [Abraham's] seed shall all the nations of the earth be blessed."

f) All Governments will Deal True Justice.
- Isaiah 11:4 "with righteousness shall He judge the poor, and reprove with equality for the meek of the earth".
- Isaiah 61:11 "…the Lord God will cause righteousness and praise to spring forth before all nations".
- Jeremiah 23:5 "A king shall reign and prosper, and shall execute judgment and justice in the earth."

g) There will be no more wars.
- Isaiah 9:6 "His name shall be called…the Prince of Peace."
- Isaiah 2:4 "…They shall beat their swords into plowshares, and their spears into pruning hooks: nation shall not lift up sword against nation, neither shall they learn war any more."

h) Health will be restored to the human race.
- Isaiah 35:5-6 "Then the eyes of the blind shall be opened, the ears of the deaf shall be unstopped. Then shall the lame man leap as an hart, and the tongue of the dumb speak."
- The only deaths will be due to and the result of sin. Isaiah 65:20 "There shall be no more thence an infant of days, nor an old man that hath not filled his days, for the child shall die an hundred years old, but the sinner [the one who died] being an hundred years old shall be accursed." If one were to die at age 100 he would have been considered to have died as a mere child.

i) The wild animals shall be tame.

- Isaiah 11:6-9 "The wolf shall dwell with the lamb…the leopard shall lie down with the kid; and the wolf and the young lion and the fatling together; and a little child shall lead them. And the cow and the bear shall feed; their young ones shall lie down together: and the lion shall eat straw like the ox… They shall not hurt nor destroy in all my holy mountain."

j) The botanical world will flourish.

- Isaiah 35:1, 2, 6, 7 "The desert shall rejoice and blossom as a rose". "…The parched ground shall become a pool, and the thirsty land springs of water…"

Revelation 20:1-3 speaks of Satan being bound with a chain and "cast into the bottomless pit, and shut him up, and set a seal upon him, that he should deceive the nations no more, till the thousand years should be fulfilled: and after that he must be loosed a little season." In verse 7 we read, "and when the thousand years were expired, Satan shall be loosed out of his prison, And shall go out to deceive the nations which are in the four quarters of the earth, …" A question that comes to mind is: "Why does God loose Satan after the thousand years of blessing that the earth enjoyed without him on the loose?" The answer is that God is allowing man to demonstrate to himself something about the natural heart of man. Though only believers go into that thousand year introductory period of the kingdom, there are many children from among the nations that are born during those 1000 years who have never been subjected to the tempting of Satan. Some of those born during that period are believers, but others are not. Satan is loosed for the purpose of revealing who is a genuine believer and who is not. It will be a testimony to the hopeless condition of the natural man that after a thousand years of blessing from God, they still will choose to follow Satan when the opportunity comes again to rebel against God. This is the tenth time that man proves his natural bent.

Man – Ten Times a Failure

1. In innocence in Eden, he follows Satan, believing Satan's lie that he can be as gods. (Gen. 3)
2. From Eden to the Flood, man is taken in by the eruption of angelic intermarriage and demonic activity in the human race in Genesis 6
3. From the Flood to Babel, man rejects God's command to scatter and instead builds an idolatrous tower to exclude God from man's future in Genesis 11
4. From Babel to Abraham, man falls into universal idolatry (Josh 24:3).
5. From Abraham to Moses, Abraham's seed was to occupy the land but instead were in bondage in Egypt until God brought them out.
6. From Moses to Christ, Israel failed to keep the law and had to be chastened often.
7. From Christ to the stoning of Stephen, Israel failed to respond to the offer of the kingdom. Three murders prove Israel's heart of rebellion.
   - In John the Baptist's death-they allowed it
   - In the matter of Christ's death-they demanded it
   - In Stephen's death-they actually committed it

8. From Paul to the Rapture, evil men and seducers wax worse and worse as men reject grace.
9. From the Rapture to the Revelation, men follow the Antichrist and fight against Christ to resist His coming to earth.
10. After a thousand years of millennial blessings, man again chooses Satan over Christ.

But in every case, a remnant believed and was saved.

The Government of the Kingdom:

1. The Lord Jesus Christ will be King of Kings (Matt. 25:31; Jer. 14:21; Luke 1:30-33. Christ will reign over all kingdoms of the earth.
2. Resurrected King David reigns over Israel (Jer. 30:9; Ezek. 34:23-26; Isa. 32:1; 55:3-4; Hosea 3:4-5; Acts 7:8; Num. 1:16; 1Chron. 22:16ff). King David will reign under Christ but over Israel.
3. The resurrected Twelve Apostles will sit on Twelve Thrones as judges over the Twelve Tribes (Matt. 19:28; Isa. 1:25-26).
4. The Twelve Tribes will reign over a Twelve fold division of the Gentile nations (Deut. 32:8; Luke 19:11-19) in which they will be a kingdom of priests (Rev. 1:6; 5:10). As a kingdom of priests, they will represent the Gentiles before God.
5. Angels carry instructions from Christ who will reign on the earth to the Body of Christ, which is now (at that time) in the heavens (Gen. 28:12-17; John 1:51; 2Tim. 2:10-12; 1Cor. 6:2; 1Thess. 4:15; 2Cor. 5:1&2).
6. All things in heaven and earth will be reconciled back to God through Jesus Christ (Col. 1:20).
7. Ultimately, all things will be delivered to the Father in a reconciled state (1Cor. 15:24).

During kingdom, the earth will be divided 12 ways. This is for the purpose of the twelve tribes of Israel ruling over the nations (Deut. 32:8).

The First Resurrection

Revelation 20:5-6

"[5] But the rest of the dead lived not again until the thousand years were finished. This *is* the first resurrection. [6] Blessed and holy *is* he that hath part in the first resurrection: on such the second death hath no power, but they shall be priests of God and of Christ, and shall reign with him a thousand years." (Rev. 20: 5-6)

This is the first resurrection of prophecy. The rapture had occurred earlier than this event by at least 7 years. The rapture included a resurrection of the members of the Church which is Christ's Body who had died but the rapture was more than that. The rapture also included a translation of living believers of the Dispensation of Grace to glory without dying. This passage (Rev. 20: 5 & 6) is back in the prophetic program and is talking about the resurrection of the believers of the prophetic program. This is the "resurrection of the just" (Luke 14:14; Acts 24:15; etc.).

The Final Rebellion

Revelation 20:7-9

"7 And when the thousand years are expired, Satan shall be loosed out of his prison, 8 And shall go out to deceive the nations which are in the four quarters of the earth, Gog and Magog, to gather them together to battle: the number of whom *is* as the sand of the sea. 9 And they went up on the breadth of the earth, and compassed the camp of the saints about, and the beloved city: and fire came down from God out of heaven, and devoured them." (Rev. 20: 7-9)

In Revelation 20:7-9, we find man's (and Satan's) last battle in their rebellion against God. This is the battle of Gog and Magog. It takes place after the 1000 year reign is over. It is precipitated by Satan after he is released from his 1000 years of imprisonment in the bottomless pit. The nations are deceived by Satan and follow him to battle against the beloved city Jerusalem. However, the outcome is quick and decisive. "Fire came down out of heaven and devoured them." It is after this final defeat of Satan that he is cast into the Lake of Fire, where the Beast and the false prophet had been for over 1000 years by then. This passage takes us back to Ezekiel 38 where God (through Ezekiel) speaks prophetically about this event. Gog is the prince of a land referred to as Magog. Some Bible scholars believe this to be Russia, based on its description as being from the north. (Ezek. 38:6, 15; 39:2, etc.) Looking at a globe, we find Moscow as being exactly north of Jerusalem. The name Meshach is suggested to be a reference to modern-day Moscow, while the name Tubal is suggested to be a reference to modern-day Tubolsheck around Moscow. However, others who have studied the demographics of the migrations of the families of nations from Genesis 10 suggest that the land of Magog is the area just north and east of the Mediterranean Sea in the area now called Turkey. This area was once part of the Assyrian empire.

In Ezekiel 38:8, we see this alliance of Persia (Iran), Ethiopia, Libya, Gomer (Germany), and Togarmah (Turkey) with Magog coming to battle against "…A land that was brought back from the sword, and that is gathered out of many people, against the mountains of Israel, which have been always waste; but it is brought forth out of the nations, and they shall dwell safely." (Ezek. 38:8) This is a description of the condition and the secure state of Israel during the Millennium. Note in Verse 11 of Ezekiel 38 that they dwell safely without walls (without defenses). Magog's intent is "to take a spoil" from the nation of Israel, which had gotten many material blessings from the Gentile nations during the Millennium (Isa. 60:9, et. al.) Note also that they came "riding upon horses" (verse 15). Note also that their weapons are (as compared with Armageddon where there is technological weaponry) bucklers, shields, and swords (Ezek. 38:4 & 5) and helmets. This is because they are coming out of the Millennium when men will have beaten the swords (weapons of warfare) into plowshares and spears into pruning hooks (Isa. 2:4). The destruction of this army will be by a great earthquake (Isa. 38:19-20) and by fire and hail from heaven (Rev. 20:9) and by confusion in which the soldiers of this army fight each other (Ezek. 38:21; 39:6). It will take seven years to pick up the weapons, and 2 months to bury the dead (Ezek. 39:9, 12).

Psalm 110:1ff speaks of the kingdom and makes the statement: "Rule thou in the midst of thy enemies…" with reference to Israel's Messiah. That means that there will be unregenerate people in the kingdom. It is here that we understand how that can be. In that 1,000 year introductory phase, there are peoples and nations that still refuse to worship Christ in spite of the lack of satanic deception and opposition. This shows the truth of Isaiah 26:10 "Let favor be shown to the wicked, yet will he not learn righteousness." Zechariah 14 tells us what will happen to the nation and the people that will not go up to Jerusalem during that time: "16 And it shall come to pass, *that* every one that is left of all the nations which came against Jerusalem shall even go up from year to year to worship the King, the LORD of hosts, and to keep the feast of tabernacles. 17 And it shall be, *that* whoso will not come up of *all* the families of the earth unto Jerusalem to worship the King, the LORD of hosts, even upon them shall be no rain. 18 And if the family of Egypt go not up, and come not, that *have* no *rain*; there shall be the plague, wherewith the LORD will smite the heathen that come not up to keep the feast of tabernacles. [19] This shall be the punishment of Egypt, and the punishment of all nations that come not up to keep the feast of tabernacles. [20] In that day shall there be upon the bells of the horses, HOLINESS UNTO THE LORD; and the pots in the LORD'S house shall be like the bowls before the altar. [21] Yea, every pot in Jerusalem and in Judah shall be holiness unto the LORD of hosts: and all they that sacrifice shall come and take of them, and seethe therein: and in that day there shall be no more the Canaanite in the house of the LORD of hosts." Zechariah 14:16-21

The Doom of Satan

Revelation 20:10

"[10] And the devil that deceived them was cast into the lake of fire and brimstone, where the beast and the false prophet *are*, and shall be tormented day and night for ever and ever." (Rev. 20:10)

Here the devil that deceived the nations is cast into the Lake of Fire where the beast and the false prophet are. They have been there for a 1,000 years. These three will be tormented day and night (no rest) for ever.

The Great White Throne Judgment

Revelation 20: 11-12

"[11] And I saw a great white throne, and him that sat on it, from whose face the earth and the heaven fled away; and there was found no place for them. [12] And I saw the dead, small and great, stand before God; and the books were opened: and another book was opened, which is *the book* of life: and the dead were judged out of those things which were written in the books, according to their works." (Rev. 20: 11-12)

The Great White Throne Judgment is the judgment of all of the lost souls of the ages. The basis of the judgment is given in Revelations 20:13 "And they were judged every man according to their works." None of those who stand before this great white throne are "redeemed". They are people who trust in their own works, rather than in the redeeming work of God or are simply people who have no interest in the things of God. The works that we find good are not the "good works" that they may have done, but the "works of iniquity". The retribution that will be meted out will be proportional to the wickedness of their deeds and the motives of the heart for "…Man looketh on the outward appearance but the Lord looketh on the heart" (1 Sam. 16:7).

A major factor in this judgment is the amount of knowledge that a soul was privy to (James 4:17; Luke 12:47-48). Works alone never saved anyone (Rom. 3:27). Under the Law of Moses, works were a required manifestation of faith (James 2:22). Today, in the dispensation of the grace of God works are a result of and not the means of acquiring justification (Eph. 2:8-10).

The awesomeness of this Great White Throne, and Christ who sits upon it, is seen and understood by the fact that both the material earth and the material heaven fled away from it. These inanimate objects, simply because they had the stain of human sin upon them, could not stand before the throne. Yet, the sinners themselves must stand before this Great White Throne, with no place to run and hide, though they would greatly desire to do so.

Seven judgments are seen in Scriptures. The Great White Throne is the last of them. When the seven judgments are completed, God's reign over the universe (heaven and earth) will be complete (i.e. All rebellion will be ended.)

The seven judgments are:

Past	1. The Cross is where all the sins of all believers are judged	Romans 3:21-25 John 5:24 John 12:31 2Corinthians 5:21 Galatians 3:13 1 Peter 2:24
Ongoing	2. Self Judgment involves our accessing our lives to conform them to Christ	1Corinthians 11:31,32; 5:5 1Timothy 1:20 1John 1:5-7
Future	3. The Body of Christ is judged for fitness to reign with Christ	1Corinthians 3:5-16 2Corinthians 5:10 1Corinthians 4:5 2Timothy 2:10-12
	4. Israelites will be judged individually and as a nation	Matthew 25:14-30 Luke 19:13-27
	5. The Nations will be judged to see who will go into the kingdom	Ezekiel 20:30-44; cf Psalm 50:16-21 Matthew 25:31-46 Luke 19:11-27
	6. The Fallen Angels	Jude 6 2Peter 2:4 1Corinthians 6:3
	7. The Great White Throne will be the judgment of the lost of the ages	Revelations 20:11-15 cf Acts 24:15

There are two sets of books present at this Great White Throne judgment.

One set is the book of the works of men. Our Lord tells his disciples, "That every idle word that men shall speak, they shall give account thereof in the day of judgment" (Matt. 12:36). Malachi 3:16 refers to this book as: "a book of remembrance was written before him for them that feared the LORD..." Ecclesiastes 12:14 also mentions a record of works "For God shall bring every work into judgment, with every secret thing, whether it be good, or whether if be evil."

The other book there is the Book of Life. All whose names are not written in the Book of Life are cast into the Lake of Fire. This Book of Life is a list of all of the Believers of the ages. Other references to it are in Philippians 4:3, Revelations 3:5; 13:8; 17:8.

There is another book called "The Book of the Living" in Psalm 69:28 "Let them be blotted out of the book of the living, and not be written with the righteous." This is apparently a running inventory record of all of those who are alive on earth at any one given point in time.

There is yet another book that Moses refers to in Exodus 32:31-33. "⁣¹ And Moses returned unto the LORD, and said, Oh, this people have sinned a great sin, and have made them gods of gold. ³² Yet now, if thou wilt forgive their sin--; and if not, blot me, I pray thee, out of thy book which thou hast written. ³³ And the LORD said unto Moses, Whosoever hath sinned against me, him will I blot out of my book." This book is God's plan for the ages - the Bible.

The Second Death

Revelation 20: 13-15

"¹³ And the sea gave up the dead which were in it; and death and hell delivered up the dead which were in them: and they were judged every man according to their works. ¹⁴ And death and hell were cast into the lake of fire. This is the second death. ¹⁵ And whosoever was not found written in the book of life was cast into the lake of fire." (Rev. 20:13-15)

Death and Hell delivered up the dead that were in them. Death held the body while Hell held the soul of the dead. Here at the Great White Throne all who stand before it are judged on the basis of their works.

Here for the first time in Scripture we find the Lake of Fire so named. It was referenced but not named in Revelation 19:20. We find it throughout the Bible though by other references. We find it referenced in Matthew 13:40 as the fire where the tares are gathered and burned. In Matthew 25:11 we find that it is the "Everlasting fire prepared for the devil and his angels". The original purpose for it was for the final deposition of the Devil and the angels that followed him in rebellion. This fire therefore would have been started before the creation of man in Eden. However, even though it had been kindled then, there is no one (neither angels nor man) who is in it today. Unsaved people today are in Hades in torment and the angels that "kept not their first estate" (Jude 6) are "... reserved in everlasting chains under darkness unto the judgment of the great day" in Tartarus (The Greek word translated "hell" in 2 Peter 2:4). Satan and the rest of his fallen angels are still free to go to and fro in the earth (Job 1:7) and to also be the principalities and powers in heavenly places (Eph. 3:10) who actively oppose believers in the world today (Eph. 6:12) and who work to keep unbelievers in darkness (Eph. 2:2). The Lake of Fire, however, will be the final destination of all lost men and fallen angels and even death and hell itself. The last enemy that will be destroyed is death (1Cor. 15:24). This is the destruction of death.

The reference to the sea as a separate place from which the dead come is note worthy. Who are the dead that are in the sea? For one thing, all of the people that perished in the flood of Noah are there. This is probably alluding to the activity of the angels which kept not their first estate in Jude 6. These angels are in Tartarus (see above). However, the offspring are in the sea.

Revelation Chapter 20 Study Guide Questions

1. Revelation 19:20 tells us what happened to the beast and the false prophet. Revelation 20:1-3 tells us what happened to the third member of the unholy trinity. What happens to him in this passage?

2. What is the bottomless pit of Revelation 20:3? Where is it located?

3. What is the antichrist's title when he goes to the pit? What is his title when later he goes to the Lake of Fire?

4. How long is the dragon bound in the bottomless pit?

5. According to Revelation 20:4, who all lives and reigns with Christ for 1000 years?

6. Is the kingdom reign of Christ only 1000 years long?

7. Why is Satan loosed after 1000 years of imprisonment?

8. Verses 5 and 6 speak of two separate resurrections. Who is raised in each? When do they occur relative to the 1000 years reign of Christ?

9. The rapture includes a resurrection. Yet it occurs before what is called the first resurrection in Revelation. How can there be a resurrection before the first resurrection?

10. What according to Verse 8 does Satan do after being released after 1000 years? Why would God release him?

11. When does man's final rebellion take place relative to the millennium?

12. Will there be unbelievers in the millennium? Consider Psalm 110 Verse 2 in your answer. How can there be enemies yet in the millennium?

13. What, according to Verse 10, is the final doom of Satan? Who was sent there (and is still there) 1000 years earlier and was still there when Satan cast there 1000 years later?

14. Who is it that sits on the great white throne of Verse 11? Why would the earth and heaven flee away from the face of it?

15. Who will stand before the great white throne to be judged? What will the judgment be based on? Will any of them pass the muster and be saved?

16. According to Verse 14, what is the ultimate disposition of death and hell? Why is the ultimate destiny of death and hell called the second death? If this is the second death, what was the first death?

CHAPTER 21

A New Heaven, a New Earth, and a New Jerusalem

Revelation 22:1-5

"¹ And I saw a new heaven and a new earth: for the first heaven and the first earth were passed away; and there was no more sea. ² And I John saw the holy city, new Jerusalem, coming down from God out of heaven, prepared as a bride adorned for her husband. ³ And I heard a great voice out of heaven saying, Behold, the tabernacle of God *is* with men, and he will dwell with them, and they shall be his people, and God himself shall be with them, *and be* their God. ⁴ And God shall wipe away all tears from their eyes; and there shall be no more death, neither sorrow, nor crying, neither shall there be any more pain: for the former things are passed away. ⁵ And he that sat upon the throne said, Behold, I make all things new. And he said unto me, Write: for these words are true and faithful." (Rev. 21: 1-5)

To understand this we go to 2Peter 3:3-10 where Peter speaks of the heavens that were of old and the earth standing out of the water and in the water. "³ Knowing this first, that there shall come in the last days scoffers, walking after their own lusts, ⁴ And saying, Where is the promise of his coming? for since the fathers fell asleep, all things continue as *they were* from the beginning of the creation. ⁵ For this they willingly are ignorant of, that by the word of God the heavens were of old, and the earth standing out of the water and in the water: ⁶ Whereby the world that then was, being overflowed with water, perished: ⁷ But the heavens and the earth, which are now, by the same word are kept in store, reserved unto fire against the day of judgment and perdition of ungodly men. ⁸ But, beloved, be not ignorant of this one thing, that one day *is* with the Lord as a thousand years, and a thousand years as one day. ⁹ The Lord is not slack concerning his promise, as some men count slackness; but is longsuffering to us-ward, not willing that any should perish, but that all should come to repentance. ¹⁰ But the day of the Lord will come as a thief in the night; in the which the heavens shall pass away with a great noise, and the elements shall melt with fervent heat, the earth also and the works that are therein shall be burned up" (2 Peter 3:3-10)

In verse 5 of 2Peter 3 Peter speaks of the heavens that "...were of old..." and contrasts them with the "...the heavens and the earth, which are now..." in verse 7. The first reference was to the heavens and earth as they were originally constituted which perished in between Genesis 1:1 and 1:2 that resulted in the earth being flooded with water and darkness being on the deep. God destroyed whatever was here on earth in the original (angelic) creation and then recreated the earth's environment to make it a suitable habitation for man. Then after 7,000 years of being inhabited by man, God will destroy it again to remake it as a suitable habitation for the redeemed of Israel and the nations to live in forever.

I refer the reader to the book by this same author entitled "Genesis from Adam to Abraham" for information on the destruction of the earth between Genesis 1:1 and 1:2. After that first destruction, God refashioned the earth to make it a suitable habitation for man. That work took six days to form the earth that we live in today (except for the modifications that occurred as a result of the flood of Noah's day and the Glacial modifications during the days of Peleg when the earth was divided).

We note that in verse 1 when the new heaven and the new earth come, there will be no more sea. We ask "Does this mean that the new earth will not have a sea or oceans? Note: It is the new heaven (singular) and the new earth that is addressed. The sea could mean (and I do think it does mean) that there will no longer be a third heaven – there will be no longer a need for it. There was no third heaven in the original creation. The third heaven came when God moved His throne off of the earth when sin and rebellion entered through the fall of Lucifer and the defection in the angelic realm. In creation week God took part of the water that covered the earth and moved it out above the heaven (the stellar universe) to form "the thick cloud" (2Sam. 22:12; Job 22:14; 26:8; Psalm 118:11-12) that hides His throne from view today.

It will the fulfillment of 1Corinthians 15:24-28 "24 Then *cometh* the end, when he shall have delivered up the kingdom to God, even the Father; when he shall have put down all rule and all authority and power. 25 For he must reign, till he hath put all enemies under his feet. 6 The last enemy *that* shall be destroyed *is* death. 27 For he hath put all things under his feet. But when he saith all things are put under *him, it is* manifest that he is excepted, which did put all things under him. 28 And when all things shall be subdued unto him, then shall the Son also himself be subject unto him that put all things under him, that God may be all in all."

Here in Revelation 21:2 we see the New Jerusalem come down from heaven. This is the fulfillment of the seventh of the Feasts of Jehovah – the Feast of Tabernacles (Lev. 23:34). The Feasts of the LORD were given to Israel to show them their prophetic future annually as they celebrated their annual sequence of feasts days. The tabernacle of God is the New Jerusalem. God will dwell with men from this point on. There will be no more death from this point on. This is 1Corinthians 15: 26 fulfilled.

The Jesus the Alpha and Omega

Revelation 21:6-7

> "6 And he said unto me, It is done. I am Alpha and Omega, the beginning and the end. I will give unto him that is athirst of the fountain of the water of life freely. 7 He that overcometh shall inherit all things; and I will be his God, and he shall be my son." (Rev. 21:6-7)

"It is done." This reminds us of the Lord's words on Calvary's cross when He said "It is finished." The over comers are here going to inherit all things. This goes back to the promises that the Lord Jesus Christ makes to the over comers in Chapters 2 and 3

The Lake of Fire and the Second Death

Revelation 21:8

> "8 But the fearful, and unbelieving, and the abominable, and murderers, and whoremongers, and sorcerers, and idolaters, and all liars, shall have their part in the lake which burneth with fire and brimstone: which is the second death." (Rev. 21:8

The fearful here in verse 8 are not the people who are afraid but rather are a reference to those who make others afraid – those who instill fear in others. There is no shame in being afraid. There is a problem though if fear makes one to compromise the truth and to refuse to stand for it. The term "death" means separation from someone or something. Physical death is the separation of the soul and the spirit from the body as we see with the death of Rachel in Genesis 35:18. This second death is the eternal separation of the lost soul from God in the lake of Fire. This is a great tragedy to be avoided at all costs yet it can be avoided at no cost to the sinner by simply by faith trusting in the Savior.

The New Jerusalem

Revelation 21:9-14

> "9 And there came unto me one of the seven angels which had the seven vials full of the seven last plagues, and talked with me, saying, Come hither, I will shew thee the bride, the Lamb's wife. 10 And he carried me away in the spirit to a great and high mountain, and

shewed me that great city, the holy Jerusalem, descending out of heaven from God, [11] Having the glory of God: and her light *was* like unto a stone most precious, even like a jasper stone, clear as crystal; [12] And had a wall great and high, *and* had twelve gates, and at the gates twelve angels, and names written thereon, which are *the names* of the twelve tribes of the children of Israel: [13] On the east three gates; on the north three gates; on the south three gates; and on the west three gates. [14] And the wall of the city had twelve foundations, and in them the names of the twelve apostles of the Lamb." (Rev. 21:9-14)

This is the city that had foundations that Abraham was looking for (Heb. 11:10). This is all Jewish. The number twelve is impressed on this city in every way. The gates had the names of the twelve tribes written on them. The twelve foundations had the names of the twelve apostles of the Lamb (Mat. 19:28; John 14:2). Note that the name of Paul (the apostle of the Gentiles) is not on anything to do with the city. Paul's eternal abode will be in the New Heavens (2Cor. 5:1) as will be ours who are saved during this present dispensation of grace.

The City Measured

Revelation 21:15-17

"[15] And he that talked with me had a golden reed to measure the city, and the gates thereof, and the wall thereof. [16] And the city lieth foursquare, and the length is as large as the breadth: and he measured the city with the reed, twelve thousand furlongs. The length and the breadth and the height of it are equal. [17] And he measured the wall thereof, an hundred *and* forty *and* four cubits, *according to* the measure of a man, that is, of the angel." (Rev. 21:15-17)

This is a sizable city. According to my estimates 12,000 furlongs is about 1377 miles. If it were placed on the land of the USA, it would occupy the area from the Mississippi River to the Pacific Ocean and from the Mexican border to the Canadian border and it would be that high.

The City Described

Revelation 21:18-21

"[18] And the building of the wall of it was *of* jasper: and the city *was* pure gold, like unto clear glass. [19] And the foundations of the wall of the city *were* garnished with all manner of precious stones. The first foundation *was* jasper; the second, sapphire; the third, a chalcedony; the fourth, an emerald; [20] The fifth, sardonyx; the sixth, sardius; the seventh, chrysolite; the eighth, beryl; the ninth, a topaz; the tenth, a chrysoprasus; the eleventh, a jacinth; the twelfth, an amethyst. [21] And the twelve gates *were* twelve pearls; every several gate was of one pearl: and the street of the city *was* pure gold, as it were transparent glass." (Rev. 21: 18-21)

There is a New Jerusalem in the eternal kingdom as well as a New Heaven and a New Earth. The nations of the earth walk in the light of the New Jerusalem (verse 22). It would appear from this that the city is not on the earth. If it were on the earth, then not all of the kings of the earth could walk in the light of it because some of the nations would be on the opposite side of the earth. The sun and the moon were not a part of the original creation but were made on the fourth day of creation week in Genesis 1. They were made to give light on the earth while the Lord was absent from the earth.

It is God's intent that the glory of the Lord would be the light of the world (Matt. 5:14; John 1:9; 3:19; 8:12; 9:5 11:9; 12:46; 2Cor. 4:4). The New Jerusalem will do for the New Earth what the sun does for the present earth. If this be true, then the sun that was made on the fourth day of creation week in Genesis Chapter 1 was only a temporary place holder for the New Jerusalem. The sun was not a part of the original creation of the heaven and the earth in Genesis 1:1 but was made on the fourth day of Creation week (Gen. 1:14-19). If the universe were heliocentric (the sun being the center), then the New Jerusalem which will take the place of the present sun will be the center of the New Heaven (the New universe).

The New Jerusalem comes after the Millennium. There is no temple in the New Jerusalem (vs.23). The temple is the meeting place between God and men. The Lord Jesus Christ is the temple of the New Jerusalem (verse 22). He is both God and man and is therefore the meeting place between God and men.

There will be a Temple on earth in the Millennium. It is described in Ezekiel Chapters 40 to 43. The temple will have to be rebuilt for the Millennium because the temple that will exist in the Tribulation will have been defiled by the antichrist (2Thess. 2:4). In fact it likely will have been built under his direction. It will be the Lord Jesus Christ Himself who will superintend the building of the millennium temple (Zech. 6:12-15). You will notice in studying these passages that the temple will not be located within the rebuilt city of Jerusalem but will be in an open area some 14 to 15 miles north of the city. This will apparently be to accommodate a large number of Gentiles who will come there to worship without having to go to the city of Jerusalem. There will be a highway from the city to the temple (Isa. 35:8; 40:3; 49:12).

Clearly there will be a City of Jerusalem that is on earth during the millennium. This city will be rebuilt and will be located in a different place than the City of Jerusalem occupies today. Ezekiel describes an area in Palestine called the Holy Oblation (Ezek. 45:1-7; 48:8, 20). The new city – The Millennial Jerusalem is in the middle of this area (48:15). The city and the surrounding suburbs cover 10 miles on each side (Ezek. 48:17). There is an area on either side of the Millennial Jerusalem that measures 10,000 reeds by 5,000 reeds that is dedicated for the production of food for the city. These are called the Possession of the City (Ezek. 48:6). There is an area 25,000 reeds wide on either side of the Holy Oblation called the Prince's Portion (Ezek. 45:7 & 8). This will extend from the west border (The Mediterranean Sea) to the eastern border (The River Euphrates). This Millennial Jerusalem will be the center of commerce in the earth (Isaiah 2:2-4; Micah 4:1, 2; Zech. 2:8-12). It will also be the center of government (Zech. 8:1-8; Micah 4:1-6) and the center of worship (Zech. 8:20-23).]

The Glory of God in the New Jerusalem

Revelation 21:22-27

> "22 And I saw no temple therein: for the Lord God Almighty and the Lamb are the temple of it. 23 And the city had no need of the sun, neither of the moon, to shine in it: for the glory of God did lighten it, and the Lamb *is* the light thereof. 24 And the nations of them which are saved shall walk in the light of it: and the kings of the earth do bring their glory and honour into it. 25 And the gates of it shall not be shut at all by day: for there shall be no night there. 26 And they shall bring the glory and honour of the nations into it. 27 And there shall in no wise enter into it any thing that defileth, neither *whatsoever* worketh abomination, or *maketh* a lie: but they which are written in the Lamb's book of life." (Rev. 21: 22-27)

There will be free access to the New Jerusalem. Anyone in the New Heaven and the New Earth will be able to come and go freely. Freedom will reign. It can because there will be no one with a sin nature to cause any problems.

Revelation Chapter 21 Study Guide Questions

1. Where in the Bible do we find the first heaven and the first earth created? Do we today live in the first earth?

2. In Verse 2 John sees the New Jerusalem come down from God out of heaven. Where are we in the time frame relative to the millennium when this happens?

3. Who is the Alpha and the Omega in verse 6?

4. What is the second death in verse 8?

5. What names were written on the twelve gates on the New Jerusalem? What names were written on the twelve foundations of the New Jerusalem?

CHAPTER 22

The River of the Water of Life

Revelation 22:1

> "¹ And he shewed me a pure river of water of life, clear as crystal, proceeding out of the throne of God and of the Lamb." Rev. 22:1

This is fulfillment of Old Testament prophecies:
Psalm 36:8 - 9 "⁸ They shall be abundantly satisfied with the fatness of thy house; and thou shalt make them drink of the river of thy pleasures. ⁹ For with thee *is* the fountain of life: in thy light shall we see light."

Psalm 46:4-5 "⁴ *There is* a river, the streams whereof shall make glad the city of God, the holy *place* of the tabernacles of the most High. ⁵ God *is* in the midst of her; she shall not be moved: God shall help her, *and that* right early."

This is the water of life that Revelation 21:6 talks about that the Lord will give to those that overcome. Revelation 7:17 refers to this stream as "...living fountains of waters..." to which the Lamb will lead the Tribulation saints. The LORD refers to Himself as "...the fountain of living water..." (See Jeremiah 2:13 and 17:13) In John 4:10-14 the Lord tells the woman of Samaria that He could give her living water that imparts eternal life.

The Tree of Life

Revelation 22:2-5

> "² In the midst of the street of it, and on either side of the river, *was there* the tree of life, which bare twelve *manner of* fruits, *and* yielded her fruit every month: and the leaves of the tree *were* for the healing of the nations. ³ And there shall be no more curse: but the throne of God and of the Lamb shall be in it; and his servants shall serve him: ⁴ And they shall see his face; and his name *shall be* in their foreheads. ⁵ And there shall be no night there; and they need no candle, neither light of the sun; for the Lord God giveth them light: and they shall reign for ever and ever." (Rev. 22:2-5)

Here we see the tree of life appear again. We saw it in Genesis 2:9 and it was mentioned again in Genesis 3:22-24 where we see that man was excluded from access to it. Had Adam then eaten of that tree, he would have lived forever in a fallen state. Therefore, God had to exclude him from it. The Tree of life is apparently a species of tree because there are a number of trees here – a boulevard of trees in the midst of the street and trees on either side of the street. The Tree of life gives twelve manner of fruit – apparently a different fruit for each month. The fruit is for healing of the nations. Ezekiel 47:9-12 speaks of a river that flows from the throne in the millennium that heals the Dead Sea and makes it productive in abundant fish life and trees on either side of it that brings forth new fruit every month and leaves for healing.

Here in Verse 3 the curse that was put upon creation because of the sin of man is removed. God cursed the ground for Adam's sake – i.e. for his good (Gen. 3:17; 8:21). Now man is in a redeemed state and can now have access to the Tree of Life and live in a creation free of the curse.

The Worship that is Directed to God

Revelation 22:6-9

"⁶ And he said unto me, These sayings *are* faithful and true: and the Lord God of the holy prophets sent his angel to shew unto his servants the things which must shortly be done. ⁷ Behold, I come quickly: blessed *is* he that keepeth the sayings of the prophecy of this book. ⁸ And I John saw these things, and heard *them*. And when I had heard and seen, I fell down to worship before the feet of the angel which shewed me these things. ⁹ Then saith he unto me, See *thou do it* not: for I am thy fellowservant, and of thy brethren the prophets, and of them which keep the sayings of this book: worship God." (Rev. 22:6-9)

"I come quickly..." indicates that this Book was written before the Lord revealed the interruption of the prophetic program by the revelation of the mystery. That means that this Book was written before Peter, James and John learned of the interruption of the Prophetic program from Paul. Therefore, this Book was written before the meeting of Acts 15. It was possibly written before or about 47 A.D. See the notes of Revelation 1:1

The Unsealed Book

Revelation 22:10-14

"¹⁰ And he saith unto me, Seal not the sayings of the prophecy of this book: for the time is at hand. ¹¹ He that is unjust, let him be unjust still: and he which is filthy, let him be filthy still: and he that is righteous, let him be righteous still: and he that is holy, let him be holy still. ¹² And, behold, I come quickly; and my reward *is* with me, to give every man according as his work shall be. ¹³ I am Alpha and Omega, the beginning and the end, the first and the last. ¹⁴ Blessed *are* they that do his commandments, that they may have right to the tree of life, and may enter in through the gates into the city." (Rev. 22:10-14)

John was not to seal the prophecy of this book. Daniel was to seal the Book of Daniel because there would be more knowledge coming by which one can understand the Prophecy. The Book of the Revelation gives the increased knowledge that Daniel 12:4 speaks about by which one can understand the prophecies of the Book of Daniel.

"...My reward is with me..." speaks of the fact that God will reward the believers of the ages for the works that they had done (1Pet. 1:4; 2Pet. 3:7).

The Open Invitation

Revelation 22: 15-21

"¹⁵ For without *are* dogs, and sorcerers, and whoremongers, and murderers, and idolaters, and whosoever loveth and maketh a lie. ¹⁶ I Jesus have sent mine angel to testify unto you these things in the churches. I am the root and the offspring of David, *and* the bright and morning star. ¹⁷ And the Spirit and the bride say, Come. And let him that heareth say, Come. And let him that is athirst come. And whosoever will, let him take the water of life freely. ¹⁸ For I testify unto every man that heareth the words of the prophecy of this book, If any man shall add unto these things, God shall add unto him the plagues that are written in this book: ¹⁹ And if any man shall take away from the words of the book of this prophecy, God shall take away his part out of the book of life, and out of the holy city, and *from* the things which are written in this book. ²⁰ He which testifieth these things saith, Surely I come quickly. Amen. Even so, come, Lord Jesus. ²¹ The grace of our Lord Jesus Christ *be* with you all. Amen." (Rev. 22:15-21)

Outside of the city are dogs, sorcerers, whoremongers, murderers, idolaters, liars, etc. This would be a reference to the Lake of Fire where all of the lost of the ages would be at this time. This is a testimony to the fact that the lost in the Lake of Fire are still there. It is also testimony to the purity and the holiness of the New Jerusalem.

Verses 18 and 19 are a stern warning to people who would mess with the Bible by adding to it or detracting from it.

Revelation Chapter 22 Study Guide Questions

1. Verse 1 speaks about a pure river of water of life. List two Old Testament Passages that prophesy of this water.

2. Verse 2 talks about a tree of life. What two verses in Genesis spoke of this tree?

3. Verse 3 says that there will be no more curse. What curse is this talking about?

4. In Daniel 12:4, Daniel was told to seal up the book. Here in Verse 10 John is told not to seal the book. Why the difference?

5. Who is giving the invitation to come in Verse 17? What are they invited to come to?

6. According to Verse 18, what will happen to anyone who will add to the prophecy of the book of the Revelation?

7. According to Verse 19, what will happen to anyone who will take away from the words of the book?

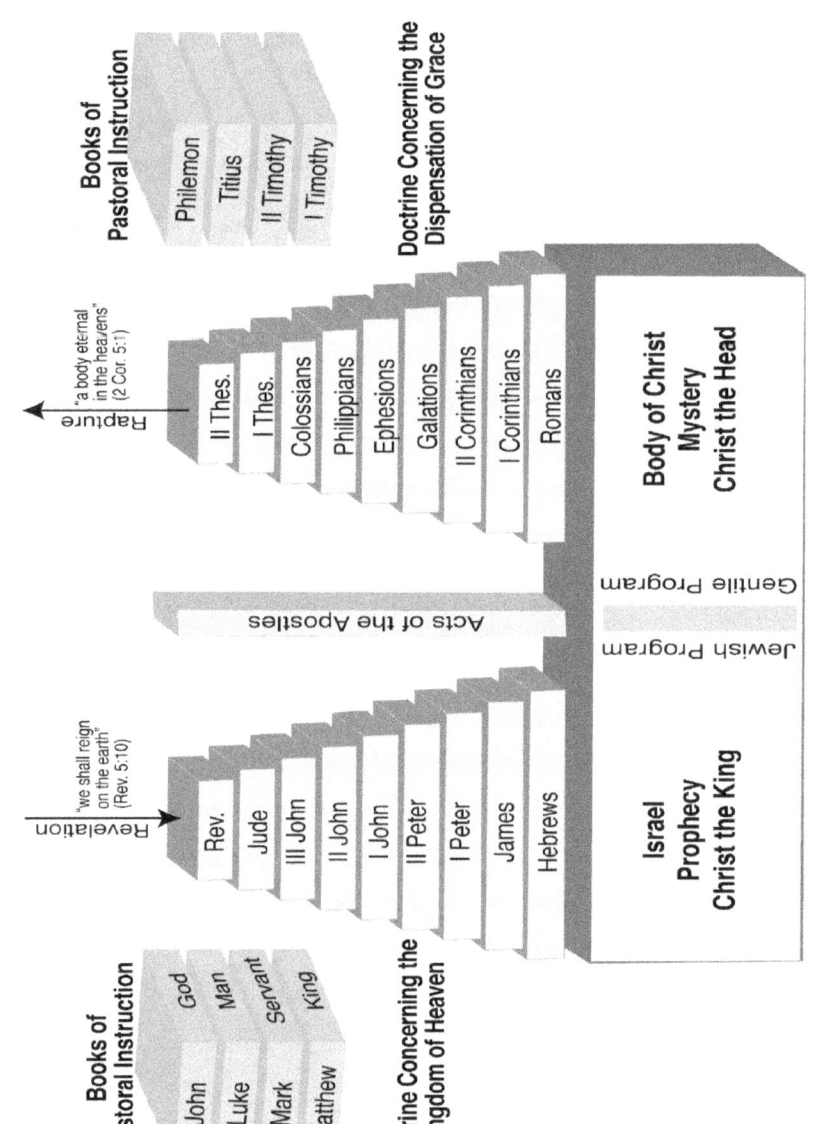

Appendix 1

The New Testament Scripture–Rightly Divided

Books of Pastoral Instruction

Philemon
Titus
II Timothy
I Timothy

Doctrine Concerning the Dispensation of Grace

Rapture — "a body eternal in the heavens" (2 Cor. 5:1)

II Thes.
I Thes.
Colossians
Philippians
Ephesions
Galations
II Corinthians
I Corinthians
Romans

**Body of Christ
Mystery
Christ the Head**

Gentile Program

Acts of the Apostles

Jewish Program

Books of Pastoral Instruction

God
Man
Servant
King

John
Luke
Mark
Matthew

Doctrine Concerning the Kingdom of Heaven

Revelation — "we shall reign on the earth" (Rev. 5:10)

Rev.
Jude
III John
II John
I John
II Peter
I Peter
James
Hebrews

**Israel
Prophecy
Christ the King**

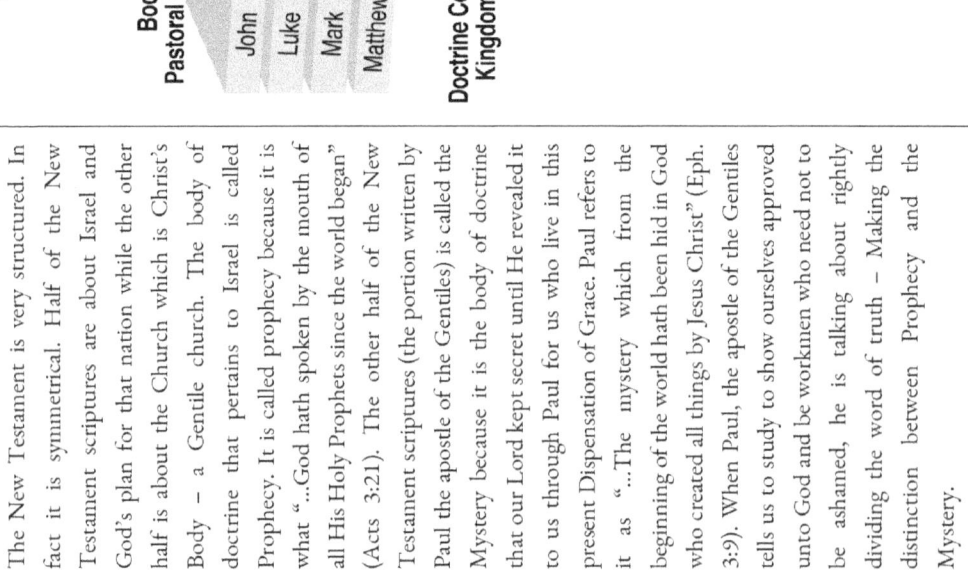

The New Testament is very structured. In fact it is symmetrical. Half of the New Testament scriptures are about Israel and God's plan for that nation while the other half is about the Church which is Christ's Body – a Gentile church. The body of doctrine that pertains to Israel is called Prophecy. It is called prophecy because it is what "...God hath spoken by the mouth of all His Holy Prophets since the world began" (Acts 3:21). The other half of the New Testament scriptures (the portion written by Paul the apostle of the Gentiles) is called the Mystery because it is the body of doctrine that our Lord kept secret until He revealed it to us through Paul for us who live in this present Dispensation of Grace. Paul refers to it as "...The mystery which from the beginning of the world hath been hid in God who created all things by Jesus Christ" (Eph. 3:9). When Paul, the apostle of the Gentiles tells us to study to show ourselves approved unto God and be workmen who need not to be ashamed, he is talking about rightly dividing the word of truth – Making the distinction between Prophecy and the Mystery.

The New Testament Scripture—Rightly Divided

	Prophecy	Mystery
Purpose	That Christ reign on earth (Zech. 9:9-11)	That Christ preeminent in all things (Col. 1:18)
Goal	A Kingdom on Earth Jer. 23:5)	A Body reigning in heaven (2Cor. 5:1; 2Tim. 2:10-12; Eph. 1:23)
Elect Agency	Redeemed Israel (Ex. 19:5 & 6; 1Pet. 2:9)	The Body of Christ (Col. 1:18, 24)
Relationship to Christ	Christ the King (Isa. 9: 6 & 7)	Christ its the Head of the Body (Eph. 1:21-23; 5:23)
Blessings to the Gentiles	Through Israel's rise (Gen. 22:18; 26:3 &4)	Through Israel's fall (Acts 28: 27-28; Rom. 11:11-15)
Relationship of Jew and Gentile	Israel Supreme (Isa. 60:1 – 3)	Jew and Gentile on the same level (Rom. 3:9; 10:12;\ cf. 11:30-32; Eph. 2:16-17)
View of Nations	Mainly concerns nation (Isa. 2:4. Ezek. 37:21 – 22)	Concerned with individuals (Rom. 10:12 – 13; 2Cor. 5:14 – 17)
The nature of Blessings to Men	Blessings both Physical and Spiritual on earth (Isa. 2:3; 11:1-9)	All Spiritual Blessings in Heavenly Places in Christ (Eph. 1:3-13; Col. 3:1-3)
View of the Lord's presence on earth	Concern's Christ's presence on earth (Isa. 59:20; Zech. 14:4)	Explains His present absence from the earth (Eph. 1:18-23)
Means of Salvation	Faith demonstrated by works (James 2:14-22)	Through Faith alone (Rom. 3:21 – 26; 4:4 & 5; Eph. 2: 8 & 9)
Relation to the Law of Moses	The Law remains in effect (Mat. 28:20 cf. 23:2; Acts 21:20)	The Law taken out of the way (Eph. 2:14-16; Col. 2:14)
Structure	Concerns God's Nation in the earth (Dan. 2:44; Mat. 6:10)	Concerns a body – a living organism (1Cor. 12:12 & 13; Eph. 4:12 – 16)
Miraculous signs and wonders	Required as evidence of faith (Mark 16:16)	Done away to be replaced with unfeigned love (1Cor. 13:8)
Apostleship	Twelve apostles, twelve thrones, twelve tribes of Israel Mat. 19:28)	One apostle to the one body (Rom. 11:13; Gal. 2: 8 & 9; Eph. 3:1-13)
Commission	Preach and baptize (Mat. 28:19; Mark 16:16)	Preach without Water baptism (1Cor. 1:17; 2Cor. 5:19 – 21; 1Cor. 12:13 cf. Eph. 4:5)
View of the Lord's Return	His return to the earth to Reign (Acts 1:11 cf. 2:36)	Return to the air to catch the Body of Christ away (1Thess. 4:17)

Appendix 2

For by him were all things created (Col. 1:16) He is before all things, and by Him all things consist		All things subdued unto Him (I Cor. 15:27) All things gathered together in Christ (Eph. 1:10)

History – God's record of the past	**Declaring the end from ancient times (Isaiah 46:20)** **I have declared the former things from the beginning (Isaiah 48:3)** **In the latter days ye shall consider it perfectly (Jer. 23:20)** **I have showed thee new things from this time (Isaiah 48:6)**	**Prophecy – God's story of the future**
The Creation of Heaven and Earth (Gen 1:1)		The New Heaven and New Earth (Rev 21:1)
The first rebellion – Satan and angels (Isa 14:28; Ezek. 28:140 The first judgment – chaos (Gen 1:2)		The final rebellion – Satan and men The final judgment – fire (Rev 21:8)
The Earth made ready for man (Gen 1:3-31)		The Earth a perfect habitat for man (Rev 22:1-7)
The first man and his Bride (Gen 2:18-25)		The last Man and His Bride (Rev 21:9-21)
The subjection to Satan (Gen 3:1-19)		The subjecting of Satan (Rev 20:10)
The Earliest Gospel (Gen 3:15) Universal rebellion (Gen 6:1-7) Judgment by water (Noah –Gen 6:8-22) The earth purged by water (Gen 7:17-24) Governments setup (Gen 9:5-7)		The Everlasting Gospel (Rev 14:6) Universal rebellion (Rev 20:8) Judgment by fire (2Pet 3:7) The floor purged (Mat 3:12) Kingdom setup Perfect Government
Institution of Babylon Idolatry invented (Gen 11:1-4) Nations scattered (Gen 11:5-9)		Destruction of Babylon (Rev. 18:2) Idolatry ended Rev 9:20; 21:8) Nations gathered (Rev 16:4; 20:8)
Call of Israel (Gen 12:1 thru Duet.) Blessing on Israel (I and II Sam) Declension in Israel (I & II Kings) Judgment on Israel (Isaiah, Jer. Ezek.)		Restoration of Israel (Rev 5:10) Judgment of tribulation Repentance of the nation (Rev 7:4) Blessing of the nation (Rev 21)
The times of the Gentiles begins (Dan, Ezra, Neh.)		The times of the Gentiles ends (Lk 21:24; Rev. 11:5)
The first advent of Christ to the manger		The second advent of Christ to the throne
Ministry of Christ The Truth His rejection and death His resurrection and ascension		Ministry of Anti-Christ The Lie His reception and reign His destruction and doom
The Spirit poured out (Acts 2:17) Second coming in view The fall of Israel		The Spirit again poured out (Rev 19:10; 22:17) Second coming in view Rise of Israel
The Mystery revealed (Eph 3) The Body called out (Eph 2:11-18) Gentiles brought in (Rom 11:16-25)		The Mystery ended with the rapture (2Thes 2:7) The Body caught up (2Thess 4:15) Gentiles cut off (Rom 11:26)

A Study in the Revelation
The End Time Fulfillment of Bible Prophecy

The Book of the Revelation is the account of the consummation of God's plan for ages. The Book of Genesis, the first book of the Bible, is the book of the origin of the universe in general and more specifically it is the divine revelation on the origin of this earth and of man's divinely appointed place in the earth. This study, *A Study in the Revelation* takes the reader into the end time events to see the ultimate accomplishment of God's eternal purpose for His creation and the revelation of our Lord Jesus Christ in glory. What started in Genesis with the creation of the heaven and the earth finally culminates in the making of a new heaven, a new earth and a New Jerusalem. There is a purpose for the heavens that is revealed, lived out in time, and consummated according to information contained in the Pauline epistles. That is all part of a divine revelation from God called "the preaching of Jesus Christ according to the revelation of the mystery" and concerns a body of believers called "the church which is Christ's body." That church will be caught up to heaven in a pre-tribulation rapture. That program for the heavens involves the present "dispensation of the grace of God" – which is basically a Gentile program. All of that part of the Bible that is outside of the Pauline epistles is in what is properly called "Prophecy." This study is a verse by verse commentary on the ultimate fulfillment of prophecy in The Book of the Revelation. This look into future events that transpire in the coming Tribulation Period teaches what is in store for God's creation in the earth and for the destiny of Israel as a nation and all of mankind in the prophesied kingdom. In *A Study of the Revelation*, the author ties those future events to the drama that has unfolded in time in human history that led up to those coming events. The Book of the Revelation concludes one leg of the two fold purpose that God has for man – that being His purpose for the nation of Israel and His plan for this earth. The other leg is God's plan for the heavenly places that are laid out in the Pauline epistles for the Gentile program regarding the church which is Christ's body. The author presents the key by which the entire Bible can be understood -- the key of "rightly dividing the word of truth." This study will bring the prophetic program for Israel and the earth together with the mystery program for us today and our future in the heavens into focus as one complete revelation for the Bible believer.

ABOUT THE AUTHOR

Michael J. Tiry came to know the Lord Jesus Christ as his personal Savior at the age of twenty-nine while in the midst of a career as an engineer. Michael served in the United States Civil Service as a professional engineer for 25 years. After 25 years with the civil service, Michael also started, owned and operated a private engineering company. While engaged in a career as an engineer, he also was involved with other men in the founding a local Bible believing church. His deep appreciation for having the assurance of eternal life, his passion for study, and his quest for truth compelled him to search deeply into the Bible with a desire to learn its truth that he might present the riches of God's grace to others. Over the last forty five plus years Michael has been involved in itinerant preaching, a church planting ministry, and a teaching and preaching ministry at Berean Bible Church in Chippewa Falls, Wisconsin. Michael also serves Berean Bible Church as director of the Timothy Institute – a Bible curriculum designed to prepare men for leadership in local churches. Additionally, Mike has been active over a span of twenty three years in a prison ministry. Michael and his wife (Linda) of forty five years have raised five daughters.

OTHER BOOKS BY THE SAME AUTHOR

Michael has written over sixteen books which are used as study guides in the Timothy Institute. This book is one of the three that has been published. Others include *"You and Your Creator,"* *"A Study in Genesis from Adam to Abraham,"* and *"More than Conquerors (recently republished as "Super Abounding Grace")."* All are available through Amazon, Barnes and Noble and other book distributors.